Putting the
Corporate Board
to Work

PUTTING THE CORPORATE BOARD TO WORK

Courtney C. Brown

Studies of the Modern Corporation
Graduate School of Business
Columbia University

MACMILLAN PUBLISHING CO., INC.
NEW YORK

Collier Macmillan Publishers
LONDON

Macmillan Publishing Co., Inc.
866 Third Avenue, New York, N.Y. 10022

Collier Macmillan Canada, Ltd.

Library of Congress Catalog Card Number: 75-14918

Printed in the United States of America

printing number

1 2 3 4 5 6 7 8 9 10

Library of Congress Cataloging in Publication Data
Brown, Courtney C.
  Putting the corporate board to work.

  (Studies of the modern corporation)
  Bibliography: p.
  Includes index.
  1. Directors of coporations--United States. I. Ti-
tle. II. Series.
HD2745.B73 1976   658.4'2'0973   75-14918
ISBN 0-02-904760-9

Graduate School of Business, Columbia University

The Program for Studies of the Modern Corporation is devoted to the advancement and dissemination of knowledge about the corporation. Its publications are designed to stimulate inquiry, research, criticism, and reflection. They fall into three categories: works by outstanding businessmen, scholars, and professional men from a variety of backgrounds and academic disciplines; annotated and edited selections of business literature; and business classics that merit republication. The studies are supported by outside grants from private business, professional, and philanthropic institutions interested in the program's objectives.

RICHARD EELLS
Editor
Studies of the Modern Corporation

STUDIES OF THE MODERN CORPORATION
Graduate School of Business, Columbia University

PUBLICATIONS

———

STUDIES OF THE MODERN CORPORATION
Graduate School of Business, Columbia University

PUBLICATIONS

———

The publication of this book was made possible
by a grant to Columbia University

from

E. M. J. Colocotronis *and* Lady Clio Crawford

–

Alexander V. Georgiadis *and* Antony V. Georgiadis
Alumni
Graduate School of Business, Columbia University

–

John M. Colocotronis

To
FRANK WHITTEMORE ABRAMS
A revered chairman of the board in his time
whose influence continues to echo through the years

Contents

Contents

Contents

Foreword

THE board of directors of the modern corporation is the helm from which one of the major institutions of our society is guided. How it is structured, how it is manned, how it is run, how it fits into the economic, social, and political fabric of our national life, are some of the most crucial issues in modern society, although they are not issues that receive adequate attention from either the popular or the academic press. Because of this, the Program for Studies of the Modern Corporation is especially fortunate to be able to publish the reflective thoughts of Dr. Courtney C. Brown, the former Dean and Paul Garrett Emeritus Professor of Public Policy and Business Responsibility at the Graduate School of Business of Columbia University, and a member of numerous corporate boards, on the need to clarify and to strengthen the role of the boards of profit-making as well as not-for-profit corporations.

The importance of the structure and function of the corporate board of directors derives from the large position of the corporation in society. At the turn of the century, J. P. Davis wrote in his well-known *Corporations:*

> The most important and conspicuous feature of the development of society in Europe and America on its formal or institutional side during the past century . . . has been the

growth of corporations. . . . Notwithstanding their vital importance to modern society by reason of their great number and increasing resources, and of the universality of their presence in the several branches of social life, corporations have shared so fully in the complexity of the growth of society during the past century that a clear comprehension of their true relations to it has not been attained.*

How right Davis was—and how prophetic. The corporation has assumed an even more dominant position in Western societies since Davis wrote, but the significance of this fact is still imperfectly understood even by most thoughtful people. In the non-Socialist world, the corporation, through which a significant part of society's work is done, has definitely become the strongest alternative locus of power against the also-widening power of the state. But where the development of the state and its government has received considerable attention for centuries, the development of the corporation and its special form of self-government has been a relatively neglected matter.

Given the natural fascination of men with the majesty. and naked power of the state, it is not difficult to understand why the state should have received so much attention. But why the concept of the corporation and its governance has been neglected is not so clear. As an instrument for getting things done, the profit-making corporation is, in many respects, the most efficient social institution yet devised by man. It has achieved this efficiency through a development that has spanned centuries.

The notion that the organizational structure of a group of citizens could have its own free-standing legal person-

*John P. Davis, *Corporations: A Study of the Origin and Development of Great Business Combinations and of their Relation to the Authority of the State*, 1897 (New York: Capricorn Books, 1961), p. 1 ff.

ality seems to have been the invention of some papal lawyers in the twelfth century. The notion was first applied to the management of monasteries, abbeys, bishoprics, universities, boroughs, guilds, and fellowships. In the vast commercial expansion that followed several centuries later, the corporate form was put to use in frankly profit-making ventures. Still later, it was the organizational and governmental form of the great industrial structures that were formed in the eighteenth and nineteenth centuries, and today still is the basis for continent-spanning global corporations that produce an increasing part of the world's goods and services.

One of the most important shifts in the governance of the corporation was noted by Berle and Means in their now classic, *The Modern Corporation and Private Property,* where they demonstrated that the direction of business corporations was really no longer in the hands of those who owned stock in them but rather in the hands of the directors and managers who were hired to operate the company. Thus, they wrote:

> As property has been gathered under the corporate system, and as control has been increasingly concentrated, the power of this control has steadily widened. Briefly, the past century has seen the corporate mechanism evolve from an arrangement under which an association of owners controlled their property on terms closely supervised by the state to an arrangement by which many men have delivered contributions of capital into the hands of a centralized control. This has been accomplished by grants of power permitting such control almost unexplored permission to deprive the grantors at will of the beneficial interest in the capital thus contributed. . . .
>
> It has been observed that under the original corporate situation there was a large amount of residual control in the shareholding group. A weakening of this control is a study by itself. . . .
>
> . . . A share of stock was once a fixed participation in property accompanied by a considerable degree of control

over that property. Today it is a participation stripped of many of its original protections, and subject to indefinite variation.†

If Berle and Means called attention to the fact that corporations were no longer directed and managed by those who owned them, John Kenneth Galbraith has gone a step further in *The New Industrial State,* claiming that the direction of the corporation is not really set by the board of directors and the top managers (many of whom, of course, sit on the board) but rather by what he calls the Technostructure. Thus, in *The New Industrial State,* Galbraith writes:

> In the past, leadership in business organization was identified with the entrepreneur—the individual who united ownership or control of capital with capacity for organizing the other factors of production and, in most contexts, with a further capacity for innovation. With the rise of the modern corporation, the emergence of the organization required by modern technology and planning and the divorce of the owner of the capital from control of the enterprise, the entrepreneur no longer exists as an individual person in the mature industrial enterprise. Everyday discourse, except in economics textbooks, recognizes this change. It replaces the entrepreneur, as the directing force of the enterprise, with management. This is a collective and imperfectly defined entity; in the large corporation it embraces chairman, president, those vice presidents with important staff or departmental responsibility, occupants of other major staff positions and, perhaps, division or department heads not included above. It includes, however, only a small proportion of those who, as participants, contribute information to group decisions. This latter group is very large; it extends from the most senior officials of the corporation to where it meets, at the outer perimeter, the white and blue collar workers whose function is to conform more or less mechanically to instruction or routine. It embraces all who bring specialized knowledge, talent or experience to group deci-

†Adolf A. Berle, Jr., and Gardiner C. Means, *The Modern Corporation and Private Property,* 1932 (New York: Harcourt, Brace & World, Inc., rev. ed., with a new preface, 1968), pp. 119, 128, 139.

sion-making. This, not the management, is the guiding intelligence—the brain—of the enterprise. There is no name for all who participate in group decision-making or the organization which they form. I propose to call this organization the Technostructure.‡

Now if the corporation is as central to society as any institution (as Davis argued), and if its management is no longer in the hands of those who would presumably have the greatest interest in its survival and success—namely, its owners—(as Berle and Means argued), but in the hands of directors and managers who are little more than the visible expression of a Technostructure (as Galbraith argues), then it seems clear that serious dangers loom for the business corporation with respect to its long-term future, both within the corporation and in terms of its relation to the demands of the surrounding society.

It is to steer the corporation clear of such dangers and to give it effective, responsive, and responsible leadership that Dean Brown has written this provocative new book. Instead of leaving the direction of the business corporation in the hands of the operating officers with their eyes only on the current year's profit and loss statement, he wants the business corporation guided by a board with interests and authorities that include, but extend beyond, an effective business operation defined by accounting periods. Ideally, such a board would include but one operating officer, the president and chief executive officer. Other corporate executives would be relieved of their operating duties after joining the board as rapidly as they could be replaced by other executives. All board members would devote their time and attention to guiding and evaluating the corporation and to relating it to the demands of the society around it.

‡John Kenneth Galbraith, *The New Industrial State* (New York: The New American Library, Inc., 1968), pp. 91–92.

Going against some recently popular notions, Dean Brown feels that adding constituency representatives from other sectors of society, especially politicized groups, can contribute little to the constructive work of the company. Indeed, he fears the politicization of the board of directors, i.e., the debating of every business decision in terms of its political ramifications. This is not to say that those without a business background cannot be valuable to the deliberations of a business board; they can be very valuable, indeed, essential if they can relate their backgrounds to the activities of the corporation and its interests and do not regard themselves simply as representatives of an identified constituency. In a society in which the business corporation is one among several major institutions, it should be restricted by its own sense of purpose and by the countervailing authority of those other institutions *from the outside, not by wrangling from the inside.*

Dean Brown's book deals with the substantive questions that must be dealt with in making boards work, passing over such issues as cumulative voting, stockholder protests, and interlocking directorates—the subjects of many recent studies—which he regards as simply not dealing with the important issues. Rather, Dean Brown discusses the requirements for achieving a "working board": a chairman with elaborated duties, an adequate committee structure, and a significant commitment of time by board members.

On the board, Dean Brown calls for a kind of Athenian democracy among the members. The president of the company would report to the board as a whole, not to the chairman; and the board would not be dominated by a single individual as is frequently the case when the jobs of chairman, president, and chief executive officer are all assigned to one man. Indeed, Dean Brown would encourage the independence of board members, not because they represent different "constituencies," but because the issues now facing corporations are so difficult and multifaceted that they require for their successful solution the consideration of a variety of openly expressed points of view.

Finally, it is worth noting that Dean Brown's analysis of the current state of corporate boards of directors and his prescriptions for strengthening them, both of which are drawn from his long experience with boards, make an important contribution to an intellectual project that needs far greater attention from scholars and businessmen, namely, the development of a theory of the firm. One might well argue that some of the problems—if not many of the problems—of the modern corporation stem from the lack of an adequate theory of the firm. The corporation is intellectually and conceptually limited by this lack of such a general theory. This is not to say, of course, that in such areas as management theory, case studies of business firms, social and economic theory, microeconomics, and operations research progress has not been made over time, but all of these parts of a possible theory of the firm have yet to be integrated.

An important part of an adequate theory of the firm must, of course, include a theory of the board of directors. Because of this, Dean Brown's analysis and prescriptions form one of the needed building blocks for the eventual establishment of the much-needed theory of the firm. The inclusion of such a theory of the board in the theory of the firm can only make the corporation better able to deal with the challenges of the present and the future.

In a world in which the board of directors has been reduced to an adjunct of management's function, Dean Brown's recommendations are bound to generate controversy. But they stem from a lifetime of involvement in the business activity of the nation and several decades of participation on a number of distinguished boards of directors. The central role of the corporation in our society demands that such perceptive and thoughtful recommendations receive the most careful consideration from the leaders of American life.

RICHARD EELLS
Director
Studies of the Modern Corporation
Columbia University

Preface

PERHAPS some kind of literary restraint should be enforced on those who have retired after a long career in business or after years of close association with it. At this time of release from the constraints of conformity that accompany a natural desire for recognition and position, books by ex-businessmen not infrequently have taken the form of uninhibited expressions of past frustrations intermingled with recollections from past experience. While one can well understand the therapeutic value of such books for the authors, they hardly contribute much to the understanding of the business system.

But other retirees, with a firm belief in the constructive contributions of business, have sought to write objectively and to set forth their insights in a sincere attempt to help assure its future healthy development. They too have often spoken their minds freely, even though there has been a modest price to pay. This thought was expressed with clarity by Clarence Randall, the much-admired Chairman of Inland Steel, writing after his retirement some fifteen years ago in *The Folklore of Management*:

> There is one caveat which must be recognized. The businessman who decides to write a book is not choosing the path of popularity among his old friends. When he speaks frankly,

as he must, not all of them will like what he says. They will point out to him sharply that criticism from outside is to be expected, but that it should never come from within the lodge itself. Even when they know what he says is true, they do not like to have such things said by one of their own.

Like Randall's, this is a book that speaks frankly. It is about an important part of the organization and conduct of both profit-making and not-for-profit corporations that makes them unnecessarily susceptible to major errors in judgment and vulnerable to attack from politicians and other sectors of the society. This is a book about governing boards that all too often do not govern. It is not so much a description of the behavior of boards of directors as it is an attempt to present a form of organization and practice that could correct some of the present infirmities.

An admirable description of present, as well as past, board practice has been provided by Professor Myles L. Mace of Harvard University in his *Directors: Myth and Reality* (1971). He concluded that boards of directors typically *do not* establish corporate policies, *do not* ask discerning questions, and, except in crisis situations, *do not* select successors to the chief executive office. He concludes that the present role of the board of directors is largely advisory.

In the few years that have elapsed since Professor Mace did his research, most observers believe that governing boards have moved in the direction of greater participation and assertiveness in the affairs of their organizations. And, of course, there are numerous political and other institutions in contemporary society that are in much greater need of repair than the governing boards of corporations. But neither of these are good reasons for not making every effort we can to improve boards of directors so that their corporations can serve business and societal interests better. This book attempts to do so by identifying and articulating the thrust toward improvement in the conduct of governing boards that has already begun as well as by extending this thinking and providing a structural outline of a revitalized board of directors.

It must be stated at the outset that the structural changes proposed here involve a challenge to a basic tenet now widely held in the business community, namely, that there can be only one head man. This is felt by many to be more important than the contrasting principle of effective checks and balances in the operations of an organization, even though the inevitable consequence of one-man rule is a subversion of the legal stipulations and responsibilities of the board as a governing body. The widely accepted premise of one-man rule leads directly to the appointment of a single individual to be both the chief executive officer and the chairman of the board of directors, that is, the senior officer of the company *and* the senior officer of the board. Now this arrangement does have some advantages for the expeditious execution of business; it may have real value for a small organization in a period of rapid growth. But its desirability is more dubious for a large, mature organization with a widespread impact on many aspects of contemporary society.

The chorus of protest about the corporation in general and about the inadequacy of the governing board in particular has become more vociferous in recent years. Unfortunately, many of the proposed reforms offered by the protesters have been of doubtful relevance. Cumulative voting, attempts to modify corporate policy through proxy voting, constituency representation on the board— all have had some influence and much publicity, but none can probably be counted on to accomplish the reforms that are needed to strengthen the corporation. In this book an attempt is made, based on more than two decades of service on various boards, to address the central problems of the operation of boards of large organizations.

The reforms suggested here are not so much proposed for rapid adoption as they are offered as objectives that it may be desirable to establish now, to be achieved over a period of time as changes occur in personnel, practice, and organizational structure. The pace in a particular corporation would depend on the traditions and past habits of the organization as well as on the people involved.

Our emphasis here will be on the board of directors of major business corporations, but we will pay some attention to the governing boards of universities, foundations, museums, hospitals, and other not-for-profit organizations, which share somewhat similar characteristics and difficulties. In Chapter 8 we attempt to identify some of the unique features of the tasks of the boards of these not-for-profit, eleemosynary institutions, the members of which are usually called trustees rather than directors.

Whether based on a corporate charter or a trust indenture, and whether members of governing boards are identified as directors or trustees, the board is the foundation on which most forms of organization are built. Members of governing boards have a prestigious status in society— more prestigious than the present nature of their activities can support. It is a status that reflects the popular belief and expectation that governing boards do indeed govern. It is the basic thesis of this book that building on that popular belief and expectation, the work of governing boards can and should be clarified and strengthened to the ultimate benefit of corporations of all kinds and of society at large.

This book might not have been written at all without the encouragement of the Director of the Program for

Studies of the Modern Corporation, Richard Eells. Both he and Philip Sporn, the former President of American Electric Power, felt strongly after reading a brief essay of mine on boards of directors that its thesis should be elaborated in a book. Generous assistance has been given in the preparation of the manuscript by numerous associates and friends, both in discussions of the thoughts presented here and in critical readings of the preliminary drafts. This has been a valuable help. Many friends in business have shared their thoughts with me over the years. It goes without saying, however, that the final distillation of ideas is the responsibility of the author.

To several in particular I am especially grateful. Parts or all of the manuscript have been read and marked by Professors John O'Shaughnessy, Eli Ginsberg, and Melvin Anshen; the last was especially meticulous in his many perceptive annotations. My largest debt is to Chauncey G. Olinger, Jr., whose careful editing of the manuscript reflected his rigorous training in philosophy and logic. If a faulty conclusion is found here, it will stem from the premises, not the reasoning.

COURTNEY C. BROWN

1

Are Governing Boards Necessary?

Some years ago a delightful book was published with the improbable title, *How to Manage a Bassoon Factory*.[1] Its first page gave away the theme: the managing director was the director who knew where the factory was. For those familiar with the operations of many corporate boards, this charming comment on managing directors makes a point that is more than whimsical.

The old adage has it that "directors direct and managers manage." What then can a "managing director" be? The pervasive point that will be made in this book will be that he is very likely the unhappy blending of the two quite distinct functions of managing and directing, of operating and evaluating. At least, that is what the managing directors of large corporations in business, academe, and other areas seem to have become in contemporary practice. This emergence of the managing director has in general meant that the independent role

[1] Nigel Balchin [Mark Spade], *How to Run a Bassoon Factory* (London: Hamish Hamilton, 1950).

1

of the board of directors has been greatly reduced, and this has happened without most of us quite realizing it or reflectively comprehending its full implications. Our purpose here will be to examine the changes that have reduced the role of the board of directors in corporate life and to suggest changes that might be made both for the advantage of business as well as of society.

According to the laws that establish them, all corporations—profit-seeking and not-for-profit—are structured with a governing board and, through their by-laws, with a managing group. Positive values can be achieved when the division of functions and responsibilities between the board and management, irrespective of the purposes for which a corporation exists, is clearly and collaboratively identified. A word about the place of the corporate form of organization in contemporary society may serve to emphasize the importance of clarifying the internal relationships between governing boards and those who are charged with the responsibility for management.

The Role of the Corporation

The corporation is by no means the only type of organization available to do the work of society, but in the more developed democracies it is the major type. There are currently three major types of organizational groupings that do the work of mankind: the family, the state, and the corporation.

The family is the smallest unit, and in many lesser-developed societies it is to this day the typical grouping that possesses the loyalty necessary for mutual commitment and effort. Because it is a relatively small grouping and the tasks of society require a wide range of abilities and interests, the family does not achieve the efficiency of more rationally organized groups. Seniority, the usual principle of leadership in a family, does not always produce the most effective direction of its activities.

At the other extreme of the spectrum is government— of the tribe, of the state, or of the nation. Here, the coercive power of the political structure, in addition to providing justice and security, becomes involved in managing economic activity. State ownership of resources and direction of community effort has appealed to many of the world's peoples as rational and desirable, but the balancing of contending parties which is so characteristic of the political process has not proven itself to be the most effective means of organizing the economic activity of a nation.

Between the family and the state, there is a vast array of voluntary associations, of which those in the form of corporations are the most important and most enduring. People in the developed democracies have turned predominantly to corporations rather than to family or government organizations for the achievement of economic as well as many other purposes of society. They have found the voluntarily assembled association, i.e., the corporation, focused on the accomplishment of consistent goals in a rationally organized manner, in practice, to be by far the most efficient use of human resources.

The results of this choice have not been disappointing. Indeed, the achievement of substantial material abundance, together with educational and cultural development in an open society, would have been unlikely and might have been impossible without the voluntary associations organized as corporations, ranging in their activities from the running of businesses to the management of colleges and museums. In this sense, the corporation, possibly more than any other influence, is the organizational form that conditions the nature and the quality of our individual lives, whether or not we actually work for a corporation.

3

Social Criticism and the Corporation

It has become commonplace to observe that the structure and attitudes of contemporary society are undergoing radical changes. The corporation, particularly the business corporation, can adapt to those changes, or it can resist them, but it cannot avoid being either a positive or a negative influence in reciprocally conditioning these changes. It cannot avoid being a decisive force—perhaps the most decisive force—in determining the character of our society today and tomorrow. "If we and our institutions are not responsive and adaptable, there is really no alternative to some of the suggestions and recommendations being made by the critics in the fringe radical groups on our campuses," Ernest C. Arbuckle, formerly Dean of the Stanford Graduate School of Business and now Chairman of Wells Fargo Trust, has said.[2]

With its own self-preservation in mind, the corporation must respond constructively to social criticism and challenge. No institution of society can maintain its vitality if it violates over extended periods the community's sense of appropriate behavior. The alternative is likely to be the imposition of additional governmental controls over corporate performance, with the ultimate probability of government ownership. This is reason enough to think very seriously about designing the corporation's internal structure and relationships in a manner to assure that it will optimally serve the public interest, which in the long run is synonymous with its own interest.

Clarification of the role of the governing board and of the desirable attributes and qualities of its members must necessarily provide the foundation on which the

[2]Ernest C. Arbuckle, "Chairman's Opening Remarks," *The Board of Directors: New Challenges, New Directions*, A Conference Report of the Conference Board, November 18, 1971 (New York: The Conference Board, 1972), p. 2.

internal structure is built. But that foundation now is anything but a firm one. A well-known corporate officer recently observed in public discussion, "Most boards of directors I have been on don't know exactly what they are supposed to do."

Should Boards Be Eliminated?

Some current opinion would disagree with the proposition that it is important to clarify and strengthen the role of the governing board. It is alleged that in many organizations the board has, in fact, been deposed by management or administrators and has been reduced to a legal fiction. As organizations grow in size and complexity, as the information requirements increase simply to maintain awareness of ongoing operations, these observers believe that the relative power of the board must necessarily shrink. Serious proposals have been made to complete the atrophy of the board, to terminate the pretense, by dissolving the board, with full responsibility and authority turned over in law to the management, as it is now, allegedly, turned over in fact. A variation of this proposal is to devise a legal way to divest the board of authority and responsibility in favor of management, except in certain clearly defined critical circumstances. But this half-way solution, because of its ambiguity, would simply shield management from the full consequences of the problems it may have caused.

Why Corporations Need Boards

There are several difficulties with these positions. First, it is simply untrue that boards in general have been deposed by management. Few boards are as inert, as supine, or as uninformed as the proposals imply. The "mushroom concept of a 'good' director," according to John T. Connor, Chairman of the Board of Allied Chemical, is a thing of the past. While a few chief executive officers still treat a good director as a mushroom, that is, "Put him in a damp dark place, feed him plenty of horse manure, and when his head rises up through the pile to get attention or ask a question cut if off quickly and decisively,"[3] most observers of the corporate scene would agree that very little of this sort of thing still exists, if indeed it ever did. Yet, many of the same observers would agree that there is a need to clarify the role of the board, and, in fact, would provide it with greater muscle.

Another reason to reject the notion of abandoning the board or reducing its influence to near-zero is that there is a potentially rewarding opportunity to achieve the positive values of a system of checks and balances through a more effective working relationship between the board and management. The board is concerned with the broad view and the long perspective more than management. Consensus decision making is most successful when a variety of points of view are represented. The major problems of today have social and political overtones; more than the experiences of a career in a single field of activity is required to cope with them. More immediate rather than long-term results are the main concern of management. Improved working procedures can and should be designed to provide better decision making by the interaction between board and management, especially with respect to what have come to be called "the externalities" of corporate organizations.

[3]John T. Connor, "An Alternative to the Goldberg Prescription," Remarks before the American Society of Corporate Secretaries, March 14, 1973, p. 4.

The Board and the Social Role of the Corporation

The broadening interest and activities of most organizations, particularly business corporations, in many kinds of societal affairs will require a parallel enlargement and adaptation of the range of concerns of governing boards. Management, historically and primarily held accountable for an efficient and profitable operation, increasingly will require support and guidance from a board with interests in a growing array of concerns dealing with the external environment: community improvement, charitable giving, employee benefits, employee health and safety, minority and female hiring and promotion, environmental protection, shareholder democracy, and even the determination of where to do business in a world of political and social tensions. "The present attack upon the incestuous cloister of corporate board rooms is the result of the confluence of all of these movements," said Patricia Roberts Harris at a November, 1971, symposium of the Conference Board; " . . . an individual who spends his or her life solely in the pursuit of greater corporate efficiency and maximizing the profits of the stockholders is somewhat removed from the day-to-day ferment of political life."[4]

The future opportunities of all types of corporations, both for-profit and not-for-profit, as institutions of societal significance can and probably should be strengthened by an attempt to identify all of the interest groups affected by corporate conduct. Of course, it will never be possible to foresee all of the consequences of the activities of major corporations any more than it will ever be possible to foresee all of the consequences of the actions of govern-

[4]Patricia Roberts Harris, Esq., "New Constituencies for the Board," *The Board of Directors: New Challenges, New Directions* (New York: The Conference Board, 1972), pp. 10, 11.

ments. Many of such consequences extend beyond the intentions or the powers of the initiators to control. But a better appraisal of probable results can be made when decisions emerge from discussion of varying points of view, and this an effectively constituted board of directors is ideally suited to do.

The Board and the Legitimacy of the Corporation

There is another reason why the governing board should be strengthened rather than permitted to atrophy. The very legitimacy of the corporation would become increasingly vulnerable to serious challenge if self-perpetuating management had no reference for continuing accountability. The central challenge now faced by corporations and their managers is the question of their legitimacy:

> The danger is that business managers don't have social legitimacy and don't know it, warns [Peter] Drucker.
> Legitimacy in this context means the corporation's right to go on doing what it has been doing for decades. . . .
> . . . business' right to set prices has been controlled by government. . . . advertising is more strictly regulated. Consumer groups have become more articulate and better organized. . . . subsidiaries of multinational concerns have been taken over by local, right wing governments. Even professional groups normally allied with the corporation are acting up.[5]

Public sanction is built on public confidence. Despite enormous corporate expenditures for "telling the story," the public withholds its full approval. The level of public criticism of the corporation seems to run in cycles. As

---

[5]Peter Drucker, cited in *Du Pont Context*, #1 (Wilmington, Del.: Du Pont, 1974).

would be expected, it was high during the great depression of the 1930s, diminished with the demonstration of corporate effectiveness during World War II and subsequently through the 1950s, and over the last decade or so has again increased conspicuously. Just a few years ago a new and relatively adequate conception of the role of the large corporation in society was developing. Today that has been reversed, and some perceive the corporation to be an economic and political threat to democracy. Tomorrow is unpredictable, but it could emerge as an uncomfortable period for the large corporation if, as now seems probable, the tensions of a slower rate of total economic growth are experienced.

In view of this, it would be prudent for the corporation to prepare itself now to make a more convincing case that its internal structures and procedures are designed in a manner to assure consideration of a wide spectrum of "publics" in its decision making. On the other hand, a further atrophy of the position of the board of directors would be the antithesis of prudence. It would leave the corporation exposed to political and public attack, to a challenge of its legitimacy that would be hard to defend against.

A Different Reason for Strengthening the Board

There is still another reason why it is now timely to clarify the responsibilities and opportunities of board members of various types of corporations. The present status of directors and trustees with respect to their personal liabilities is at best ambiguous; some think it to be ominous.

The typical dictum in state charters provides that "the business of a corporation shall be managed by its board of directors." If taken literally, there is no board member of a large organization in the nation who could feel secure. Fortunately, *state* legislatures and judges have accepted the reality that management responsibility must necessarily be delegated to full-time corporate officers. The states have been much criticized for permissive regulation of board members' responsibilities, improperly in my view, for it is doubtful that the development of what is now called professional management would have been possible if a different position had prevailed.

The forfeit of the board's chartered responsibility to manage the day-to-day affairs of the company is no fault; it is realistic and desirable. A similar forfeit of the board's obligation and responsibility to guide, supervise, and evaluate is quite another matter. The first forfeit would seem to involve no measurable personal risk. The second involves large personal risks as evidenced by the rendering of numerous judgments in recent years by *federal* courts in cases brought under the federal securities laws.[6] Strict standards have been promulgated for accurate disclosure in key public documents such as press releases, proxy statements, annual reports, and registration statements. If the material signed by a director turns out to be inaccurate or fraudulent, he can be held accountable even though he may have relied on assurances of the organization's executive personnel. Or he may find himself guilty of negligence even though care is taken to be fully aware of the facts if he fails to make unfavorable information publicly known. These are risks that have begun to emerge that are beyond those of participation in fraud, transactions involving conflicts of interests, and "inside trading."

The governing board can protect itself from these haz-

[6]Securities and Exchange Commission v. Texas Gulf Sulphur Company; Escott v. Bar Chris Construction Corporation; and Securities and Exchange Commission v. Mattel.

ards only if it participates more fully than at present in the background development of the organization's activities and care is exercised in supplying directors with operating information that is adequate in quality and quantity. As things stand, the liabilities of directors weigh more heavily than their influence on the running of the corporation. Redressing the balance could not fail to be constructive, both for the board member and for the corporation.

Governing Boards *Are* Necessary

Proposals to diminish still further the role of the board are based in part on the false notion that governing boards now have a minor role to play. That is simply not so and, indeed, the trend in recent years has been toward a greater assertiveness by boards of directors. The need for the board's participation, moreover, is increasing as corporations become more complex and their activities affect larger numbers of people. A clarification of the board's role and responsibilities is necessary for numerous reasons, of which a clear understanding of personal liabilities is only one, even though an important one. Instead of a further weakening of the board's position in the corporate structure, a substantial strengthening is desirable to provide the benefits of checks and balances, an optimal blending of harmony and challenge, as well as a commingling of specialized expertise with broad understanding and social perception in the organization's decision making.

Yes, an unqualified yes, is the answer to the title of this chapter. Governing boards *are* necessary. The chapters that follow will examine some of their opportunities and explore some of the structural patterns and procedures that may be helpful in achieving those opportunities.

11

2

Governing Boards of Business Corporations

Directors of business corporations now live in a world of ambiguity—some have said of myth—with regard to their legal status. For example, the relationship between a chief executive and his fellow board members—for rarely is the former not a director—is determined only in part by legalities; it is also a matter of personalities, of organization history, and of intermittently changing situations, which may include the redistribution of share ownership in a stock company. The relationship differs from company to company and from time to time, and is conditioned by the size of the organization and the nature of the business or activity in which it is engaged.

Likewise the organizational structures and procedures of boards are almost never identical. A full description of the variations would simply be confusing. What we will do here is identify certain basic principles, practices, and problems of the boards of large non-financial stock corporations as a background to offering a number of suggestions for improving corporate performance through a strengthened governing board. Some of these suggested modifications to current board structure and practice should provide a bench mark from which adaptations may be considered.

It will not be easy to describe these modifications without bruising sensibilities, for any substantive change in existing patterns would involve reassignments at the highest levels of corporate officialdom. Yet, in the long run, clarification and strengthening of the role of the board of directors as an institution may be crucial for the continued healthy development of the corporation as a major constructive influence in an open society. Mr. Roger M. Blough has expressed it very succinctly:

> . . . the search for a better way of conducting every aspect of corporate activity is never ending. There is no reason, therefore, why improvement in the work, protection, and general usefulness of outside directors should not be an integral part of this search. Like everything else, the functioning of boards is not beyond examination or above reproach and possible improvement.[1]

Just as no two boards are exactly alike in their traditions, procedures, and practices, the processes by which change can be achieved most effectively will differ from board to board. Personalities will no doubt dominate some situations. Some will prefer to invoke grandfather clauses and make changes only with a changing of the guard. Others, less satisfied perhaps, may feel it imperative to seek improvement of a board's structure and functioning without delay. As early as 1966, the Chairman of the Board of Texas Instruments urged a "deliberate structuring of our board and its operating procedures [to provide] a badly needed coupling between the rapidly

[1]Roger M. Blough, "The Outside Director at Work on the Board," *The Record of the Association of the Bar of the City of New York,* Vol. 28, No. 3, March, 1973, p. 203.

changing external and internal environments."[2] Still others would prefer a deliberate period of reflection and contemplation before revising the board's work. The latter would, of course, be the least painful. Even those who now oppose any change might find a period of reexamination useful.

There may be, however, some peril in excessive delay. Those campaigning for the conversion of the corporation from a private to a public or quasi-public institution hang their case in part on what they perceive to be the "unrepresentativeness" of the board of directors. The board, it is alleged, represents only itself, not even the stockholders of the company. Since it is dependent on management's favor for the selection of its members, the board is in no position to function as an independent agent. The challenge to its legitimacy is frequent among reformers, who hold that a basic change in the allocation of power within the corporation is required to correct the situation.

Some of the suggested remedies, such as electing public, government, or special interest representatives to the board, conceivably could simply create internal political conflict to a degree that would make the board's functioning even more ambiguous, and by delay, indecision, and inaction, make it even less effective than it is at the present. Some allege that interest group representation cannot impair board effectiveness since they believe that most boards are already ineffective. A certain amount of divisiveness may, conceivably, make the board more visible, but by its nature, the board is not and cannot become a full-blown legislative body without destroying the capacity of the corporation to fulfill its traditional functions effectively.

[2]Patrick E. Haggerty, "Remarks," *First Quarter and Stockholders Meeting Report*, April 18, 1973, Texas Instruments Incorporated.

One-Man versus Consensus Management

Probably the basic reason why boards have been exposed to the charge of a lack of independence is that their functions have not been clearly defined and kept separate from those of management. The rational way to restore a sense and, ultimately, a tradition of independence to board members is to strengthen the position and role of the board by distinguishing it from management, both in function and in membership. To be meaningful this would have to start at the very top with the chairman of the board and the chief executive officer.

In recent years the practice has grown of electing a single individual to the several posts of chairman of the board, president, and chief executive officer, thus making a single individual the senior officer both of the board and of the company. A variation is to elect one person chairman of the board and chief executive officer, and another, president and chief operating officer. In both cases the head man is confronted with the difficulty of separating out his functions and responsibilities as the chairman of the board from those he holds as the chief executive of the company. *The ambiguity of the role of the total board begins right here.*

The merits of this concentration of authority, however, should not go unnoted. It does focus in one individual ultimate authority for policy determination and for the initiation and administration of a program of action. This arrangement streamlines and expedites decision making and helps to assure prompt implementation. When a single individual is the senior officer of the board *and* of the company, it becomes virtually certain that the program and the tone of the organization will become an expression of his attitudes and aspirations. The resulting effectiveness has given wide currency to the belief that a

15

successful company can have but one head man. And, indeed, this arrangement can be beneficial to the company, and through the company, beneficial to society at large.

Or it can be—and on occasion has been—swiftly calamitous; a single major blunder of judgment can damage an enterprise seriously. It would be interesting to know the extent to which write-offs, ranging from $100 million to $500 million, that have been recorded in recent years by such well-known companies as Anaconda, Ford, General Dynamics, Occidental Petroleum, RCA, and United Aircraft stemmed from the dominant influence of one decision maker. Or, in a different type of situation, a head man's prolonged lack of imaginative leadership or judgment can result in a gradual erosion of the organization's vitality over a number of years. The rise and fall of great corporations over extended periods of time as well as the sudden, unexpected catastrophes of others are all too familiar to students of business history.

The advantages of concentrated authority are more likely to be realized in the young and rapidly developing business, especially if the leader is a person of capacity, imagination, courage, and energy. The same is true in situations that have deteriorated to a point where they need the resuscitation that can be supplied only by a strong new hand at the helm. In both of these general cases, the justification for one-man control stems directly from particular circumstances, one the initial development of a business, the other the reestablishment of the healthy condition of a business. Readiness to take great risks and the capacity for quick and decisive action are important to success in both cases, although even here it should be recognized that there is the possibility that these risks can also result in disaster.

The large mature corporation, on the other hand, presents quite a different set of circumstances. The processes of decision making have come, of necessity, to involve large numbers of people. The impact of the decisions made in the large established corporation cannot but affect both those within and those outside of the company. Indeed, what have come to be called the "externalities" of the business corporation have now begun to appropriate the time and energies of executive management of the large corporation to a point that the operation of an efficient and growing business can be jeopardized. Managing the mature modern corporation in a complex and rapidly changing world involves a task that is getting beyond the capacity of a single mortal. The chief executive officer, especially of the mature corporation, is entitled to guidelines prescribed by the board that extend beyond simple "bottom-line accounting" and that reflect the total, widely based experience of a carefully selected board of directors.

As we examine this issue of whether individual management or consensus management is the more suitable for the mature corporation, a distinction must be made between the authority over *all* the affairs of the large corporation and the authority over the operating functions of the business. It is now common practice to lodge all authority of running the business, both internally and externally, in a chief executive officer who in turn delegates the responsibility and the authority that goes with it to designated officers throughout the organization. The extent of the delegation depends on the nature of the activity and the disposition of the chief executive officer involved. Where authority for all the affairs of the company are delegated to the chief executive officer, the board of directors then acts more like an advisory committee than a body of ultimate authority. Consensus management, on the other hand, would involve identifying those authorities delegated to the chief executive officer and those retained by the board, just as the chief executive officer now identifies those delegated by him throughout the organization from those he retains in his own office.

The issue of concentrated versus distributed authority is characteristic of all organized groups. It is not a matter of one pattern being bad and the other being good in some absolute sense. Rather the issue should be resolved pragmatically in terms of the purposes in view. In the case of the government of the United States, Americans identify distributed authority with democracy, and hence call it good. Other peoples, in different stages of development or with different traditions, reject this aspect of the democratic process in the United States. On the other hand, in another area of activity, such as a football game, authority to call the signals is given to the quarterback, or to the coach on the bench acting through the quarterback. The point is, whether in government or football, the authority structure followed is that judged best to achieve the goals of the group. There must be a recognized and accepted method to initiate decisions on behalf of the group, transmit decisions to the group, and finally make the decisions effective through group effort.

In the case of the U.S. government, initiatives leading to decisions may originate in the House of Representatives or the Senate (depending on their nature), in the executive office of the President, or in the executive departments. The legislative and executive branches check and balance each other, and the final arbiter is the judiciary. The system is a bit clumsy and there are those who question its capacity to cope with the complex and rapidly changing circumstances of the present, even though it has recently demonstrated impressive resiliency.

Similarly, many will doubt that the authority to make the complex decisions required of a large modern corporation should, or can, be distributed *between* the board of directors and the management. The question is whether there are significant types of decisions that can be identified and segregated, decisions for which the board and management, respectively, would have the *initiating* responsibility.

True, there are not clear and distinct breakpoints in the continuous and interrelated progression of purchasing, processing, transporting, warehousing, and marketing; and the business skills of financing and accounting affect all of these activities. Price determinations are involved at every stage. A business is an integrated and continuous whole. Unless consciously guided, its operations from day to day probably do as much—and possibly more— to mold a company's policy as do the governing board's efforts to provide a prior blueprint for the direction of the company's development. In other words, a case can be made for keeping or placing the locus of all final decision making in one place, in the office of the chief executive officer who may happen also to be chairman of the board. But a case can also be made—and in the instance of the large corporation perhaps a better one—for identifying types of decisions, and for distributing authority for their initiation between management and the board.

The strength of our form of political democracy is in its system of checks and balances more than in the rule of the majority. As the modern corporation confronts the progressively more complex problems of what has been called the post-industrial era, it will stand in progressively greater need of the advantages of a system of checks and balances within its own operations. Technology is changing rapidly, the scarcity of raw materials and their rising real costs foreshadow a slower rate of economic growth, corporations are spreading their interests around the globe, labor is changing in its attitudes and aspirations, and the public at large is expecting corporations to participate in, if not to spearhead, the community search for a better quality of life. The capabilities needed to guide the business corporation henceforth must be social and political as well as technical and economic. This is an agenda of interests that involves more than the continuous and integrated processes of a traditional business operation. Indeed, an attempt by a corporation to accept an expanded range of responsibilities without internally modifying its organization to deal with them could be counterproductive and frustrate the ability of the corporation to perform its traditional functions.

Efficiency and productivity improvement have been the great strength of the corporation. They are and must remain the distinctive task of management. This is a task properly delegated by the board and, apart from appraising results, should be left entirely to management. But it is too much to expect management to be all things to all people. Management watches—and is judged by—the "bottom line," which measures the return on investment. Actions expressing the social responsibility of corporations most frequently—although perhaps not always—involve a departure from this principle of maximizing the return on investment; and this departure cannot reasonably be expected from executive management, at least to any great extent or on a continuing basis.

When the Founding Fathers incorporated the idea of the separation of powers into the Constitution, they defied the conventional wisdom of the day that accepted the divine right of a king. We may now be at a stage in the development of corporate purposes and governance that requires the same level of imagination and courage to assure the future healthy development of an institution that has been the major builder, and now stands at the center, of our industrial society. It may be time to separate the "legislative" functions of the board from the "executive" functions of management and to establish a clear demarcation of the membership of the two groups. The ability of the corporation to adapt to the larger public expectations of the future may depend on it.

In summary, the long-term development of the corporation can be secured better by designing procedures for checks and balances between management and the board in their determination of the major directions of its internal activities. This will require a strengthening of the board in its participation and collaboration with management in certain identified functions. The exercise of a guiding role by the board in the external relationships of the corporation can be meaningful only if the board possesses the influence and prestige derived from a stronger position in overseeing the internal affairs of the corporation. Great care must be exercised, however, to preserve management's opportunity to maintain executive initiatives, flexibility, and control within predetermined guidelines.

The Legalities of Transition

There are no legal impediments to strengthening the position of the board. The dictum in state charters that the corporation "shall be managed by a board of directors" can only mean that general control and direction of corporate affairs and the supervision of the corporate officers, to whom the day-to-day management is delegated, belongs to the board. Technically, directors are elected by the voting stockholders of the company to represent the interests of stockholders with due diligence and prudence. Even though it is not typically by a conscious action, the board then collectively reserves certain types of decisions to itself and delegates other types to management. Legally, it is that simple.

The public now generally assumes that, after election by stockholders, the major tasks of a director are to participate in the selection of competent people to manage the company, including the chief executive officer or officers, and to make a reasonably continuous and comprehensive review of its operations. Another responsibility that is generally expected of a director is that of participating in establishing broad guidelines for administering the assets of the enterprise in a manner to serve the interests of the stockholders and the public at large. Not so generally recognized is the responsibility to guide the company's course into channels that will provide future fruitful development and profitable operations. Such long-term considerations may, in some circumstances, stand in contrast with management's interest in maximizing profits in a given year or years; thus, it should especially be the business for the board.

The Election of Board Members

This description of the election and functions of corporate directors is admittedly truncated and inadequate. Indeed, relative to the process of electing directors it borders on the fictional. For the most part, interim additions to the list of directors now are identified and selected by the chief executive officer for formal approval at a meeting of the existing board members. Suggestions for nomination may or may not be solicited from fellow officers of the company and from other directors, but additions unacceptable to the chief executive officer are usually unthinkable—and under normal circumstances probably should be. They are then reelected by the stockholders' proxies at the annual meeting; in substance, this "election" is merely a confirmation.

In recent years some companies have changed the procedure for nominating new members for the board. For example, General Motors some years ago established a nominating committee of six outside board members. The committee was made responsible for preparing a list of potential additions to the board, for reviewing the possibilities with the chief executive officer and other directors, and, subsequently, for bringing the new names to a meeting of the full board for further discussion. In addition, this nominating committee was authorized to determine the total number of board members to be elected.

Another example of revised procedures for selecting new board members is provided by Allied Chemical. A subcommittee of the board, consisting of three outside directors, has been created and given very broad powers. They have been given the authority to review the general responsibilities of the board, its functions, talents, compensation, *and* membership, as well as its organization, structure, size, and composition, and then to advise and make recommendations to the full board on these matters.

There are instances, no doubt, in other companies in which the procedures for additions to the board have been formalized; but it is the more general practice that an informal suggestion of a new name is made by the chief executive officer, perhaps in consultation with one or two of his older board members, for later submittal to the full board. It is a recommendation that is seldom contested.

The method of cumulative voting as a means of adding new members to the board has been much debated; perhaps more than it deserves. Where it has been adopted by voluntary action or by state legislation, it seems to have had little influence. Even if it is possible to get one or two representatives of an interest group elected to the board by the cumulative voting method (casting all of a shareholder's votes for a single candidate or a few candidates), the election of a small minority to the board is unlikely to change policies or programs—and, in fact, it has not done so in a significant sense.

The important consideration is the control of the proxy machinery. Some have found an anomaly in management's control through proxies of the very process through which its nominal superiors are elected. It is held that in fact the proxy process in today's stockholders' meeting and the physical convening of a scattering of stockholders is more in the nature of a charade to conform to the required legal formalities.

The Termination of Board Membership

Procedures for the termination of board membership are likely to be even less formalized than those for the election of new members. Apart from a predetermined but variable retirement age, they are likely to be related to the desires of the chief executive officer. As most boards now function, an excess of independence can make a board member's position uncomfortable. A board member should be insulated from unwarranted retribution. The sudden discovery by chief executive officers of a dissenting board member's alleged conflict of interest in outside associated activities has not been without precedent.

On the other hand, no management can be expected to function saddled with independently minded board members whose persistent position appears to be that of an arbitrary or capricious adversary. Members of boards tend to be experienced and in their senior years. Self-confidence in their own views may be strong. The confidence of younger members may be just as strong, unencumbered as it may be by the possession of experience.

The matter of independence of posture among board members cannot be disassociated from competence and incompetence. Methods should be available to the board itself to deal with incompetence among its members in whatever form it may take, or whenever it may appear in a member's incumbency. This is a delicate matter that may strain mellowed friendships, but it must be dealt with if the work of the board is to be revitalized and if the board is to perform a more significant role.

Ways should be devised, in which executive management need not participate formally, for boards to self-prune their membership when it becomes advisable. The development of an orderly and well-understood procedure to do so within the operating procedures of the board would alleviate some of the hurt feelings involved.

It may be safely said that despite legalities to the contrary, stockholders as a group in normal circumstances typically play no meaningful role in additions to or deletions from boards of directors.

The "Four Ps" Identify the Board's Concerns

Policy, personnel, procedures, and *performance* have been called the "four Ps" for the proper attention of board members. Together, they constitute the hard core of the governing board's responsibility to stockholders, who, as a legal matter, elect them to board membership. In examining these responsibilities it is important to note that many authors have called attention to the disparity between myth and fact in the present functioning of boards.

The process of *policy* formation, generally assumed to be a function of the board, has now become as management controlled as the selection of board members. If policies are discussed at all, they are usually proposed by management and presented to the board for brief review and endorsement. Seldom does a member of the board propose a basic change of policy for board discussion and approval without first obtaining the informal endorsement of the chief executive officer.

The wellsprings of policy formation at present are more likely to be the successive investment and operating proposals presented by management to the board. These proposals, drafted in the various departments of the corporation, waft implicit policy from below upward to the board for its approval. Such operating programs are now more influential in determining the directions of an organization's development than are the more generalized statements of policy and purpose that might emerge from prior board discussion and approval.

The range of interest in *personnel* implied by the legal status of directors extends beyond its own incumbency to the selection of senior company officers. Here again, the function is now fulfilled more by management than by the board, including the senior officer's selection of his own successor. The development and monitoring of administrative *procedures* that would assure a comprehensive and detailed review of performance is usually also left to management. But this should be another responsibility of the board, at least to the extent of reviewing the procedures after they have been developed. The board's concern with a review of *performance* is a major task. This is now perhaps the most adequately fulfilled of the board's functions, but the depth, regularity, and frequency of review is not always sufficient to assure that the board is fully informed.

It should be observed, moreover, that the concerns that influence policy have been substantially broadened in recent decades. Stockholders now share with other publics the attention of both board members and management. Consumers, labor, and the communities in which investments are made and operations occur, all have interests that in the long run are recognized as being functionally intertwined with the long-range interests of stockholders. The policies and regulations of federal, state, and local governments, in general and in detail, describe standards to which the corporation's activities must reasonably conform. This widening range of corporate interest in several publics and in general public purposes has been based less on altruism than on a conviction that a balanced recognition of the impact of the company's activities on all the parties involved will best serve the future development of the enterprise.

The Board's Role in Social Responsibility

A still further enlargement of board concern, if not a yet universally felt responsibility, has been emerging in recent years, again no doubt in the conviction that it is in the future interest of the corporation. Starting several decades ago with the financial support of educational and cultural activities, boards of directors and managements of corporations have progressively extended their interests to include various means of improving the quality of life in general; their concerns have gone beyond simply providing satisfying jobs and material abundance. Indeed, they have gone beyond the stipulations required by law.

It is too soon to conclude that these relatively new expressions of "social responsibility" are fully *accepted* responsibilities, although they have been given visibility with much writing and oratory. And while there have been many instances of self-imposed restraint on profit maximization to prevent public harm or displeasure, at present, such matters as ecology and conservation, personnel development, and the alleviation of poverty and discrimination must be viewed only as tentative responsibilities, except to the degree prescribed by law.

Since executive management is held accountable primarily for profits, these responsibilities probably will become generally *accepted* in the sense of extending beyond the minimums required by law only after board members are able and willing to identify and impose a very long-range view of the company's interest. Thus another major responsibility of the board, over and above the matters of policy, personnel, procedures, and performance, which are internal to the company, is to give management encouragement and guidance in matters related to such external opportunities. Management is usually ill-equipped for the purpose.

Professor Kenneth R. Andrews has written:

> . . . good works, the results of which are long term and hard to quantify, do not have a chance in an organization using conventional incentives and controls and exerting pressure for ever more impressive results.
> . . . The internal force which stubbornly resists efforts to make the corporation compassionate . . . is the incentive system forcing attention to short term quantifiable results.[3]

Still further away from the matter of legal or accepted responsibility, but nevertheless of growing interest to

[3]Kenneth R. Andrews, "Can the Best Corporations Be Made Moral?," *Harvard Business Review,* Vol. 51, No. 3, May–June, 1973, p. 61.

some directors, is the participation by businessmen in the formulation of national economic policy in collaboration with government officials; in the establishment of guidelines for prices and wages in a setting of continuous inflation; in formulating a program, for example, for the continuance of a vital service such as the northeast railroads; or in the clarification of appropriate degrees of competition and monopoly in national and international trade in an increasingly aggressive world. Participation in the political formulation of national and international economic policies, however, must be viewed as another tentative responsibility except in the case of the multinational corporation that must necessarily help in reconciling conflicting legislation in different national jurisdictions.

Perhaps as important as collaborative action with government is the opportunity for businessmen in general to participate actively and forcefully in evolving public debates on the major social and economic issues of the day. No organization that plays an important role in society, nor the representatives of such an organization, can escape that responsibility, although, admittedly, it is sometimes difficult to determine whether the individual spokesman or the organization of his affiliation is heard when he or she speaks or writes.

Clarification and Collaboration of Board and Management Functions

In a period of growing complexity, to give a simple definition of the work and responsibilities of directors and executives, respectively, would be not only difficult, but very likely inadequate. The functions of both may change as external or internal circumstances are modified. One distinction is essential, however, to the effective discharge of the board's collective responsibilities and for the future healthy development of the corporation: the board of directors is the proper body for the establishment of broad policies and procedures and for reviewing senior personnel and performance; management personnel are selected by the chief executive officer in collaboration with the board and delegated to carry out these policies and procedures with effective performance.

This distinction is not widely accepted in contemporary corporate practice. Rather, the reverse is true. Management sets the objectives, strategies, and policies, and then brings them to the board for approval. As Professor Myles Mace of Harvard University discovered after extensive inquiry, boards of directors do not typically establish objectives and policies, audit performance thoroughly, ask discerning questions, or even choose a chief executive officer except in crises. As one chief executive officer recently observed: " . . . one of my primary functions is to make sure that the majority of the board of directors are aware of who, in my opinion, should take the company over if I get run over by a truck."[4]

The distinction above between the board and management has legal validity and, if observed, provides a better bench mark than the state charters to help resolve the troublesome matter of where the board interest diminishes and management interest appears. There is, of course, no sharp line that defines this matter, nor is it desirable that one be drawn. There are some issues that are appropriately reserved for board decisions. There are others that through delegation have become, over the years, clearly management functions. In between, there

[4]Harleston R. Wood, cited in "The Essential Board Function," *The Board of Directors: New Challenges, New Directions,* A Conference Report from the Conference Board, November 18, 1971 (New York: Conference Board, 1972), p. 23.

are still other matters that constitute a band of responsibilities of major concern to both board and management.
A general distinction between board and management
responsibilities, fortunately, can help sort out the matter
of which group has the responsibility for *initiation* in the
specific issues that arise in this band of mutual interests.

The problem of clarification, although seldom de-
clared, is present in every boardroom and executive
suite. It is illustrated by the resignation of Arthur Goldberg from the board of TWA. Denied a staff and a budget
with unlimited access to company records, Mr. Goldberg
deemed himself unable to discharge the legal requirements of a director's responsibility. Management, on the
other hand, could not but feel inhibited, if, having been
assigned the task of running the enterprise within prescribed goals, it is continuously audited by individual
board members, or by the board as a whole, prior to
appropriate reporting periods.

The delegation of authority and responsibility is a
cardinal principle of good management. Many executives
take great satisfaction in their ability to develop young
managers by delegating administrative authority and responsibility as far down the line as possible without jeopar-
dizing effectiveness. This is the essence of "industrial
democracy," and a board should be willing to maintain a
proportionately greater trust in its senior management.

It must be recognized, however, that restraint by the
board exposes it to the danger of being inadequately
informed of unfavorable developments. The collapse of
the Penn Central provides a glaring example, and
numerous others have come to light in recent years. Put
in another way, restraint by the board imposes a clear
burden on management to disclose fully the unfavorable—
including its own mistakes—along with the favorable
features of its operations. Failure to do so is clearly a

breach of the trust placed in management by the board, and it provides grounds for reconsidering the suitability of retaining those responsible for the withholding. Without an open and complete flow of information between management and the board there cannot fail to be an impulse, shared by Mr. Goldberg, to probe independently into the areas delegated to management. But there is a prohibitively high price to pay for such probing.

Apart from prior approval of purpose and subsequent review of results, it must be recognized that there is real danger in intervention by a board. It can be—and has proved to be—debilitating. While board members with prior business experience are not likely to concern themselves with operating details and become a harassment, it is true, however, that, through thoughtless practice by both directors and managers, there has tended to be an undesirable degree of blurring of the appropriate distinctions between the work of the board and management. Dual appointment of one person as chairman of the board and chief executive officer has made a major contribution to that blurring.

Another aspect of the blurring is that, often, members of company managements other than the chief executive officer also serve the organization as board members. They are commonly known as inside directors. They can provide valuable inputs for the work of the board. If their numbers predominate, however, the old cliché of "operations make policy" will come into full play, and the opportunity to check and balance operations against policy will be lost.

The confusion can be avoided if officers of the company are relieved of all operating responsibilities and of their titles as soon as possible after joining the board. This may not be feasible during a transition period, simply because most companies, including some large ones, do not have the management talent to spare. But the objective is a good one and if approached gradually, by reducing company assignments and enlarging board assignments, the separation of officers of the board and officers of the company can be achieved over time. The one exception would be the president and chief executive officer, whose function is to manage the total activity. When senior executives are removed from daily operations after joining the board, they then are no longer inside directors as that term is now understood, but rather members of the board with a rich fund of knowledge and experience about the company's affairs.

Even a partial recognition of the distinction between the board and management personnel has helped to clarify the work of the board in some corporations. Such a distinction has helped to sort out the respective functions of an officer of the company, on the one hand, and of an officer of the board, on the other. The former is epitomized by the chief executive officer or president, and the latter by the chairman of the board. Texas Instruments provides an interesting example. In addition to the chairman and the president, board members are divided into three categories: general directors, directors, and officers of the board. Both the chairman and the president are employees of the company, but their primary responsibilities are to the board and to the company, respectively. General directors are expected to spend as much as 30 days annually on board affairs and directors as much as 15 days. Their compensation would approximate $1,000 a day. Neither general directors nor directors are employees of the company. Officers of the board are employees of the company who will retire fully from operations in a few years—perhaps at age fifty-five—with the expectation of becoming general directors.

The practice of drawing board members from senior

operating officers of the company has another precedent, even if the nomenclature is slightly confusing. The Standard Oil Company (New Jersey), now Exxon, for years was said to have a totally inside board even though the board members, recruited exclusively from executive officers of the company, were relieved of all operating responsibilities after election. Their task was to help develop policy and procedures, and to counsel with operating officers of the company in the review of personnel and performance. In recent years, several outside directors without company experience have been added.

It might be observed that organizations that are not so large and complex as Exxon and Texas Instruments would find it difficult to achieve these arrangements. In addition to their scarce management talent, relieving an executive officer upon election to the board of all operating responsibilities could leave him with less than a full work load and create problems of compensation. This could circumscribe the company's opportunity to have available on its board the experience and wisdom of career employees. Encouraging former company officers after election to the board to engage, on a limited basis, in appropriate outside activities, including membership in public service organizations and on other company boards that do not involve a conflict of interests, should alleviate these difficulties, including those of compensation.

Moreover, a board composed of non-company directors and former operating officers need not be denied the counsel and experience of its current executives. Operating officers who are not board members can always be invited to join in board discussions on appropriate occasions. This participation in board discussions prior to possible election to the board can provide current directors with very useful opportunities to evaluate the qualifications of an operating officer for such election.

There is nothing in the division of functions between members of the board and officers of the company to imply conflict of purpose or adversary relationships between the two, except perhaps to the extent that management is more concerned with short-term performance and the board is perhaps looking further ahead. Quite the contrary, it is in the interest of both to seek arrangements that can help the organization to limit its mistakes without impairing the initiative required to develop successfully through time. Arrangements that clarify the respective functions and responsibilities of the board and management, and provide a system of checks and balances that will minimize mistakes and maximize successes, cannot fail to make a positive contribution in the long run.

On reflection, many of the strong leaders now vested with extensive responsibility both as chief executive officer of the company and chairman of the board would probably welcome a bifurcation of their pinnacle position and would prefer to have less leverage on the activities of their boards. Among the results would be a wider distribution of responsibility and some relief from a typically punishing work load. As a by-product, the greater participation of board members in guidance and consultation in depth could reduce the not inconsiderable fees now paid to outside consultants.

Mr. Robert M. Estes, Senior Vice President of General Electric, observed at the highly informative Conference Board symposium, *The Board of Directors: New Challenges, New Directions,* in November of 1971:

> The roles of senior management have developed to the point where an intimate working association with outside board members is a logical imperative built into the management system itself. . . . directors as a class are the only voluntary means remaining to provide the objectivity, perception, independence and over-all accountability essential to safeguarding the credibility, and therefore the viability, of

our major business enterprises and ensuring their responsiveness to social as well as economic imperatives.[5]

A similar view has been expressed by Professor H. Igor Ansoff of the European Institute for Advanced Management in Brussels. He believes that the post-industrial era poses awesome challenges for the future manager and a single human will no longer be able to carry the full burden of general management responsibilities. "The culturally ingrained American concept of placing full authority and responsibility in one man will give way to shared decision-making."[6]

The underlying issue is whether decisions of a nonroutine nature are to be made by the executive office, usually by a single individual serving both as the chairman and chief executive officer, and then confirmed by a passive board, or by a process of rigorous group examination and discussion by independently minded, but commonly dedicated, board members including the chief executive officer. In the interest of good hard policy and conclusions, it is important to examine a reasonable number of independent and penetrating challenges to all proposals before reaching a consensus of the board and management. Professor Irving L. Jarvis has expressed succinctly the importance of independent and uninhibited discussion by identifying the source of defective judgments among the various clusters of decision makers surrounding U.S. Presidents. His observations are apropos of our discussion of boards of directors in business.

Over and beyond all the familiar sources of human error is a powerful source of defective judgment that arises in cohe-

[5]Robert M. Estes, "Liability and the Director," *The Board of Directors: New Challenges, New Directions*, p. 14.

[6]H. Igor Ansoff, cited in "Changing Styles of Management," *Du Pont Context*, #1 (Wilmington, Del.: Du Pont, 1974).

sive groups of decision makers—the concurrence-seeking tendency, which fosters overoptimism, lack of vigilance, and sloganistic thinking. . . .

The more amiability and esprit de corps among the members of a policy-making in-group, the greater is the danger that independent critical thinking will be replaced by groupthink, which is likely to result in irrational . . . actions.

Jarvis also has observed that:

A group whose members have properly defined roles, with traditions and standard operating procedures that facilitate critical inquiry, is probably capable of making better decisions than any individual in the group who works on the problem alone.[7]

Although it is recognized that the involvement of a board of directors tends to increase at a time of change or trouble, it is not enough that it reacts to problems after they have occurred and are presented by management for consideration, discussion and, hopefully, resolution. By definition, good administration must be anticipatory, must foresee problems before they occur, must put out small fires before they become big ones. A vigorous and independently minded group of board members, presumably with extensive experience in a broad range of public and private activities, can serve as an early warning system to avoid difficulties, even catastrophes, that otherwise might occur. This has become increasingly true as external influences of a political and societal nature have more and more affected the activities of the corporation. As one commentator has colorfully expressed the point, the board, "sitting higher on the crow's nest than the crew on the deck, can see the rocks ahead a bit more clearly."

To achieve these results, board members must be fully informed, and they must be able to confirm to themselves

[7]Irving L. Jarvis, "Groupthink in Washington," *New York Times,* May 28, 1973, p. 15.

that independence of position is desirable—and desired. If board members, due to a lack of definite procedures for receiving information, are not aware of all the relevant facts or of alternative courses of action, or are required to act on significant proposals without adequate time for preparation, the result will necessarily be an unbalanced domination in the decision process by those more familiar with the background of the proposals, namely, the operating managers. In many instances, that may itself be a disservice to management.

How Much Independence?

How much independence in directors is desirable? Surely an excess of independence could become intolerable. One answer is that the extent of legally imposed responsibilities on the board and the degree of independence of board members should be more positively related. One of the reasons for the disinclination of qualified men and women to join boards is that the responsibilities imposed are now felt to be out of balance with the independence that is desired or tolerable on many boards, with the result that the exposure to personal liability is excessive.

In recent years, a number of judicial decisions have enlarged the requirement of prudence in a director. Federal courts have held that board members must now be fully informed, ultra-careful regarding possible conflicts of interests, and scrupulous not to use inside information for personal benefit. They must develop more than a cursory knowledge of the company and the field or fields in which it operates. They must confirm the accuracy of important reporting documents such as registration statements and proxy material. Self-dealing, inside trading, and conflicts of interests are subject to heavy penalty. Any one or several of these requirements, if violated, can be accompanied by large liability. The more important point, however, is that all of these requirements are also necessary if a board member is to function in a positive, objective, and independent manner, and reach intelligent conclusions.

While most chief executive officers no doubt welcome the idea of a board as advisors with different but relevant experience and points of view, not all of them could be expected to embrace a shift in the present balance of power between management and the board that has evolved over the years. Their point of view here may not be so much a desire for personal power as a conviction that committee management is poor management. They are aware that more has been learned about professional management and administrative structure, making it possible for organizations to grow in size and complexity, which has made it increasingly difficult for board members to participate meaningfully.

Yet it is doubtful, because of external and internal pressures, that the existing relationships that typify board and management can be sustained; indeed they are now and will continue to be for some time in an active stage of reexamination and modification. Failure by executive management to take a positive stance in the invigoration of the board and clarification of its functions invites a high risk. External interests are becoming increasingly assertive in their clamor for reform of the corporation as a central institution of contemporary society, and they are focusing much of their attention on the board of directors. Activists among stockholders have already made their influence felt. The federal government and the courts have not been disinterested. Indeed, case law is moving discerningly toward standards of care and awareness that cannot be attained with present practices. In theory, the federal securities laws are intended to require more complete disclosure; in practice they have become a means of giving visibility to the performance of directors.

Finally, scholars have begun to look more closely at the board of directors. What they are now writing is not flattering. It will not enhance the status of the corporation. If management can find within its own strengths the determination to devise ways to revitalize the institution of the board of directors, even at the cost of surrendering some of its own authority, the result will be far more rational and constructive than if it waits until the changes are forced on the corporation by external influences. The greatest danger facing the business community is that many businessmen fail to recognize the public's increasing appetite for government regulation, and even control.

3

A New Job for the Chairman

THE division of responsibilities between the board of directors and the management of a company advanced here implies a revision of our current concept of the role of the chairman of the board. Although in most cases he would be identified and elected by the board after a successful career in the company—but not necessarily as chief executive officer—on becoming chairman he would no longer be an officer of the company. He would then be the senior officer of the board, to which he would give his primary allegiance. Beyond this his constituency would be the management, other employees of the company, stockholders, and the whole range of external publics that now affect the corporation.

In the board proposed here, the chief executive officer of the company, that is, the president, would not report directly to the chairman of the board but rather to the collective board, of which both he and the chairman would be members. They would have equal status in the sense that neither would report to the other as a sub-

41

ordinate. A clear delineation of their respective functions would be the foundation upon which they would build and sustain a harmonious relationship.

The Functions of the Chairman

The chairman should have two principal functions. First, he should make certain that the board is properly discharging its responsibilities. It should be his task—not that of the chief executive officer—to guide the organization of the board and determine what the board collectively does and does not do. Among his responsibilities he should assure that all board members are adequately informed. He must be a consummate negotiator. In its broadest outline, his job should be to encourage the process, and, in the long run, the tradition, of consensus decision making by a group of independently minded board members in collaboration with management, a process in which the chief executive officer should fully share, but which he should dominate only to the extent of his more intimate knowledge.

Second, the chairman should relieve the chief executive officer of the company and his operating associates of some of the excessively heavy burden of representing the company to its external publics: consumer groups, environmentalists, certain government agencies, business associations, institutional investors, even Wall Street analysts. Unlike some who have been identified in the past as "Mr. Outside," the chairman would be a spokesman with recognized internal authority and prestige; a public agent of the company with intimate knowledge of its affairs and with influence within and outside the company.

Specific Tasks of the Chairman

A simple recitation of the range of specific tasks for which the chairman of the board should have initiating responsibility is impressive. If done adequately and effectively, this work would require a major time commitment. In collaboration with the chief executive officer, he would:

1. schedule meetings of the full board and its several committees;
2. organize and present the agenda for regular or special board meetings;
3. review the adequacy of documentary materials in support of management's proposals that are sent to all board members for their study in advance of meetings. Alternatives that may have been considered should be disclosed;
4. assure adequate lead time for the effective study and discussion of the business under consideration;
5. take under continuous review the flow of information to and from board members.

Subject to the full board's review and approval, he would:

6. propose to the board for its approval a committee structure together with the assignments of fellow members as committee chairmen;
7. assign specific tasks to members of the board;
8. establish procedures to govern the board's work;
9. prepare and distribute proxy material to stockholders;
10. most importantly, in collaboration with his fellow directors, identify guidelines for the conduct of the directors and assure that each is making a significant contribution.

The board's work usually should be handled in the office of the chairman. Specific matters might originate with him, or be referred to him by the president or by a committee of the board. Occasionally, they might originate with an individual board member. The range of the chairman's activities related to committees of the board will be elaborated in Chapter 5, "Organizing the Working Board."

When a task appropriate to the board's responsibilities has been identified by the chairman, background documentation should be developed by a designated board committee, usually with the assistance of the internal company staff and the company officers involved. The documentation would be prepared under the supervision of the chairman's office if the matter falls outside a committee's designated interest. The matter would then go on the agenda of a meeting of the full board, with or without recommendation. The submission by management or the chairman of a proposal for consideration without recommendation should not imply disapproval, but rather that, in the specific instance, a discussion without prejudice by the full board is desirable.

Informing the Board

The point is often made that business organizations are poor communicators. The development of orderly procedures to assure adequate communication between management and the board, between the board and the external publics of the company, and between the board and the company's stockholders should occupy a significant part of the chairman's time.

The main concern underlying Arthur Goldberg's proposal was a feeling of uncertainty about the adequacy of the flow of information from management to the board; in the words of the old saw: "It isn't what I don't know that bothers me; it's what I don't know that I don't know." He would have assigned a separate staff to an overseers committee of the board with the funds to commission outside consultants when necessary to assure a comprehensive inquiry into all major proposals and their alternatives. The infirmities of the Goldberg proposal have been exhaustively presented, including the challenge it implies to the principle of delegation based on confidence. While the Goldberg proposal has problems, there remains, nevertheless, the widespread current practice of management typically serving as both advocate and judge when a new course of action is presented to the board for approval.

A procedure developed cooperatively by the chairman and by the chief executive officer, using company staff, would be a preferable and less disturbing means than the Goldberg approach to assure that all board members are comprehensively informed of the full range of thinking and analysis, including possible alternatives, that has preceded the appearance of an item on the agenda.

There can be no doubt that interposing any procedures for more thorough information dissemination to the board than is current practice would involve some delay; how much would depend on the procedures. This may be the price paid for greater certainty. To one chief executive officer it would be unacceptable: "If you have someone other than the chief executive officer filtering everything through to the board, it would be an almost impossible situation to try to operate under." Yet one of the major difficulties that faces boards of directors today is the problem of being fully informed. Without this, the values of the board's breadth of experience and wisdom are at least partially immobilized, the strengths of checks and balances are lost, and management, acting as both advocate and judge, simply cannot escape a bias in its position even though it may be unaware of it.

Numerous other means are available to inform board members more fully. The development of a committee structure, with each committee assigned to report back to the full board on specific areas of interest, can concentrate attention on different phases of the company's activities. It is important, however, that these committees of the board be chaired by officers of the board and not by officers of the company, so that, again, operations do not dominate policy.

Company staff should be used to develop background data, after the chairman and the president have determined which staff members are available and qualified. Opportunities for a board committee to be in contact with the company's external counsel and accounting organization, however, should be recognized and encouraged as a normal procedure. The chairman of the board, of course, should be kept fully informed of the work of these committees. In turn, he should serve as a bridge to keep the chief executive officer informed.

Various other means are available to the chairman to assure that board members are familiar with company affairs. Organized plant visits, management seminars, and attendance at social functions all provide an opportunity to make the board more familiar with company personnel and the nature and nuances of the company's activities. It is a matter for judgment in each case how much time can or should be assigned to these out-of-meeting activities, but present practice no doubt assigns less time than should be the case.

The most obvious means of informing the board, of course, is through reports, letters, memoranda, bulletins, etc., delivered with adequate lead time. Their effectiveness depends on their nature. Manifestly, they should be both concise and comprehensive; only long enough to cover the pros and cons of the main points at issue succinctly. The chairman can perform a highly useful role by informing management about the types of material that board members find most useful and the types that are redundant.

The Chairman as External Communications Officer

Another type of communication that should appropriate a major share of the chairman's attention concerns the company and its several external publics: security analysts, environmentalists, leaders of minority and youth groups, consumerists, academics, and other molders of public attitudes, including officers of government. This he would do both personally and indirectly through his fellow board members. Most members of the board, with the chairman's encouragement, should participate personally in public affairs in one or more ways in order to bring to the board's deliberations a sensitive awareness of external influences that now is too often missing. The chairman should facilitate these external associations of his fellow board members in numerous ways, construing the time spent on them as "company time" when appropriate and providing normal expense allowances. In a sense, this practice could constitute an alternative to special interest representation on the board. At the same time, it would strengthen the posture of the corporation at its weakest point; specifically, it would help to maintain on the board a sensitive awareness of the social changes occurring in society.

Stockholder activities present still another area of communication about which the chairman should have a direct concern. Church related funds and the endowments of foundations and universities have put pressure on managements in recent years to follow various policies that have no direct relation to profitability, the stockholders' traditional interest. Indeed, programs have been urged that would reduce immediate profits. Procedures for presenting stockholders' proposals have been established by the Securities and Exchange Commission's regulations for proxies, but there remains an insistent pressure for the development of formal procedures for review of such proposals within the company.

Institutional investors, on the other hand, have shown little interest in influencing management, preferring to keep their position flexible so that they might liquidate a holding if dissatisfied. This posture may prove to be illusory if larger percentages of a company's total outstanding issues are accumulated, making liquidation difficult if not impossible without destroying values.

A third category of stockholders, the rank and file investor with holdings ranging from an odd lot to a thousand shares, is also typically passive with respect to pressure on management. An occasional letter to the company is usually handled with a reply prepared, and sometimes signed, by a member of the secretary's office. But the growing activism of church, foundation, and university groups, and of groups specifically organized to use stock ownership to bring pressure on management, and the potential pressure of the "locked in" institutional investor, all point to the growing importance of providing a ready channel of communication from the top levels of a company. The chairman's office is the logical place to locate this activity.

The Proxy Process

Another function of the chairman should be the supervision of the proxy process in collaboration with his fellow board members, including the chief executive officer. This task should be carried out with a clear recognition that control of the proxy process by executive management has been one of the features of corporate practice most subject to criticism. It is alleged that through control of the proxy process, the chief executive officer of the company determines who will be the members of the board and thus assures himself a friendly panel of "bosses." By shifting control of the proxy procedures to a committee of the board under the general guidance of the chairman (who is not at the same time the chief executive officer), this source of attack by critics of the corporation can be substantially reduced.

The Chairman's Job

From this recitation of the chairman's assignments and activities it should be clear that they should relate to general corporate matters and to board review of its activities—not to operations. Indeed, the chairman's only influence on operations would derive from his membership as one individual on the board. The chief executive officer of the company would be the authorized manager of the business, subject to the policies and review of a board of directors of which he also is a member.

It goes without saying that a harmonious relationship would be an essential requirement between two individuals, each holding ultimate responsibilities in designated areas of activity that are by their nature interrelated. The achievement of harmony between two rational and intelligent individuals so situated has much precedent, however, and it is reasonable to anticipate it if the respective areas of responsibility are clearly delineated. A team approach by which decisions emerge through consensus becomes the normal pattern after the transition is completed. But if a certain amount of friction should develop during a period of transition from what has been called "one-man rule" to the procedures of consensus decision making, the cost may be a modest price to pay for the greater strength of a secure organization.

A final word should be said about the new and extended job of the chairman as it is described in this chapter. Today there is a tendency to hold the total board responsible for assuring that procedures exist for a comprehensive flow of significant information from management. Some feel that recent interpretations of the federal securities laws have created intolerable risks of civil liabilities. Practical limitations make it difficult for board members to learn of or prevent conduct that may give rise to a legal action. It is uncertain how the courts would interpret an expanded role for the chairman as a major channel of communication between the board and management. It should not be prejudged whether his exposure to liability would be greater and that of other board members lessened. It can only be observed that all board members, including the chairman, now share the exposure to civil action, and it is reasonable to expect that organizing the board better to assure an adequate flow of information for the fulfillment of its responsibilities should mitigate some of the total risks involved.

4

A Full Job for the Chief Executive Officer

THE *Business Week* issue of May 4, 1974, carried an extensive study of the chief executive officer, his world, and his activities. The study was headed with a provocative caption: "Chief Executive: Facing outside forces for which he was neither trained nor selected." In the introduction to the series of articles, *Business Week* stated:

> At a time when the CEO is already under pressure because the company he runs has grown so vast and the economy so tumultuous, he is being told to take on a major new function: that of envoy from the corporation to the world at large.

The chief executive officer was trained and picked for actually managing a company, and running the business of a major corporation is a full-time job in itself. But *Business Week* reports,

> The corporate woods are filled with companies in trouble because the CEO was not minding the store. Yet if the CEO shirks his role as social arbiter, the assaults being directed

against business today could prove so intense that they might well force a fundamental change in the nature of the American corporation.[1]

The Duties of a Chief Executive Officer

A succinct description of only some of the duties that are now involved in "managing a business" is sufficient to confirm the large demands and heavy responsibilities that are imposed on the chief executive officer of a major corporation. It is these now enormous duties that are implied by the seemingly simple stipulation of state legislatures, expressed in their corporate charters, that the board of directors shall manage the business. These duties have now, of course, been delegated by the board to management as personified by the chief executive officer—and properly so.

First and foremost, his duties include making and keeping the enterprise healthy, that is, profitable, and, if at all possible, growing through internal investment or external acquisition. This should be accomplished, along with all of the other matters involved in running a large and complicated business, within the purposes and limits determined by the board. He must develop an administrative structure that is adapted to the nature of the business and yet one that retains the flexibility to change as the business changes. Under his general supervision, personnel programs must be designed that will apply to the bench worker as well as to his immediate associates in the executive office, all geared together to achieve a harmonious meshing of human talents and skills. New employees must be selected and trained, and current

[1]"The Chief Executive Officer," *Business Week*, May 4, 1974.

employees must be shifted, advanced, or pruned from the working force.

The chief executive officer must assure supplies and secure markets. He must attend to changes in inventories and to the behavior of his receivables. When difficult situations arise, he is called upon to "put out fires." He must make certain that the company's operations are compatible with legislation and regulatory law. Only rarely can he or his executive associates escape dealing directly with labor unions. Reliability in the internal preparation of financial reports to the investment community must be one of his continuous concerns.

He must supervise the preparation of an annual operating budget, broken down in detail for each operating unit, to guide managers throughout the organization. Long-range planning, often in the form of a moving five-year operating target that discloses future needs for capital and other resources, must be carried on continuously and reviewed for conformity to the policies of his board. All of the company's financial resources must be made to do the maximum amount of work at all times, without standing stagnant either as float or unrequired deposits. Sound and secure financial management to assure the capability to seize opportunities for unusually favorable acquisitions when they appear is a continuing concern of the chief executive officer.

The Organizational Structure of the Corporation

The administrative structure of the company must be one that will get all of these things done. And to know whether they are done or not, the chief executive officer must create the channels for a reliable and prompt internal flow of financial and operating information, both up and down the organization. Whether the traditional hierarchical pyramid will be the most effective means of control or whether his organization must be supplemented with a system of task forces for specific purposes, or even whether decision making should be diffused among plural centers, is a matter that he must judge perceptively.

Moreover, none of these are one-time activities on his part; arrangements must be continuously reviewed and modified. And it must be recognized that greater interest and involvement by the board will make the task no easier. There is little wonder that *Business Week* and other observers of the corporate scene are beginning to question whether managers, who in fact have neither trained themselves for, nor been selected for, an additional range of newly emerging external tasks, should—or can—be expected to do or be all things for all people at all times.

A further insight into the activities of the chief executive officer is provided by a brief review of the typical organization of a business firm. It is a system of substructures, usually called departments, arranged pyramidally, peaking in the chief executive office. This structure is familiar and includes the line departments of purchasing, production, manufacturing, transportation, warehousing, and marketing, as well as the staff departments of accounting, finance, personnel, public relations, law, etc. This structure is typical of all manufacturing corporations; in other types of business organizations it is varied to adapt to one special situation or another. But, by and large, most business organizations are now fundamentally similar.

This line and staff structure has been designed over many years through trial and error; it has proven effective in maximizing efficiency in routine and repetitious operations. In an environment that is above all competitive, it is a stable and predictable arrangement. And yet this kind of a structure, and the control and incentive systems that are embedded in it, can tend to inhibit rather than encourage initiative and change within the organization. Equally important, they can tend to focus attention on short-run results. Because of this, one of the tasks of the chief executive officer is to find the means of offsetting the typical influence of "corporate bureaucracy" and instilling a sense of drive, self-reliance, and purpose throughout the organization that some call vitality, others initiative.

The Increasing Operational Demands on the Chief Executive Officer

Factors such as accelerating product obsolescence are beginning to compel more frequent modification of organizational arrangements. The importance of imaginatively introducing new products is of course increased as product life cycles become shorter. The fact that expenditures on research and development have continuously increased as a percentage of total expenditures on plant and equipment assures a continuous flow of new products. Moreover, markets are rapidly changing; some are growing, some are stabilizing, and some are contracting. And markets are becoming global.

New methods of business decision making, supported by the mathematics of operations research and the fast information retrieval and computation capability of the computer, now require a level of management sophistication previously unknown. Whether one is concerned with new products or with a logistics system of procurement, production, sales, and inventory control, these new abilities now cut across the normal departmental life of a corporation. Indeed, it has been said that formerly reliable constants used in the consideration of difficult problems have now become galloping variables.

All of this leads to the simple recognition that all the operating functions of a business are interrelated and need the close and continuous attention of the chief executive officer. Into his thinking must go prices, costs, sales volume, profit margins, investment needs, plant capacity, consumer habits, and many other variables. Sharply drawn departmental lines and programs must necessarily be supplemented and indeed modified by the overview of senior management and, ultimately, by the chief executive officer.

This is a conclusion that is reinforced by the fact that the complexity of the corporation and its economic environment now generate an increasing number of "special projects" internal to the company. Better abilities must be developed to *anticipate* purely business problems as well as to resolve them after they have appeared. The organizational response to such problems will require a grasp of new technology and new analytical methods as well as a vision of new tasks and markets for the company. The need for the continuous testing of deep-rooted convictions based on past operating experience will be personal as well as corporate.

The Demands of the Corporation's External Environment

All organizations, including business organizations, respond to an external as well as an internal environment. If the demands from the internal environment are strong, even more insistent demands for adaptation derive from the changing nature of the environment in which business operates. And in this external world, the

56

organization—whether it is a business organization or otherwise—must continually deal with new facts. It is in meeting these new demands that the chief executive officer needs—and can rightfully expect—the initiative of his board.

Economic considerations not immediately related to the internal processing, servicing, and selling of goods and services have, in recent years, appropriated a progressively larger amount of the time and attention of the chief executive officer. The quality of the local environment in which factories and offices function, typically within the cities, is deteriorating. Business is called upon to cope with these problems, and the public expects it to help solve them. Government restraints in the field of antitrust are becoming more numerous; more cases are being prosecuted. Constraints imposed by labor law and labor relations are being multiplied. Consumer and environmental groups have succeeded in obtaining new regulatory legislation. Maximum economic growth with reasonably stable prices—a government policy on which business has relied for a quarter century—has more recently become, in a period of emerging shortages and alarming inflation, a hollow incantation of bewildered economists. Consumerists and environmentalists are joined by security analysts, an array of officers from government agencies, and journalists, all claiming a share of the chief executive officer's time.

It is clear that new and distinctive corporate abilities are now needed and will be needed even more in the years to come. The means must be found for the development of new initiatives within the organizational structure of the corporation if it is to make a positive response to the changing environment that is both prompt and effective. The time and attention of the chief executive officer must not be appropriated by these external demands to the neglect of his operating responsibilities.

57

The externalities of business, as important as they are, must not be allowed to impair the capability of the corporation to get its basic work done.

Beyond the internal activities of the corporation, these external demands now being made on business will require changes in organizational structure and new assignments of authority. The tasks that loom ahead are far too complicated for one man to grasp. As Arjay Miller, former President of Ford, now Dean of the Stanford Graduate School of Business, has said, the chief executive's job simply is becoming "too much for any man to handle."[2] Indeed, the staff of a whole department of a corporation is unlikely to possess the competence to deal with the complexity and difficulty of many of these problems.

It is little wonder that a plaintive cry is heard from the chief executive officers interviewed by *Business Week* for its May 4, 1974, issue. Let the chief executive officers speak for themselves: "The amount of work necessary to prepare yourself and keep informed about the political situation, the world situation, and how investors are reacting is terrific. And it keeps getting bigger." Twelve-hour days for chief executive officers are not uncommon. "The chief executive has switched from a long-term planner to a short-term thinker." "It is easy to go from crisis to crisis and let long-term planning slip." On the other hand, "It would be easy to spend all your life on external problems and not really get into how the organization is functioning." Yet, "The chief executive must take a position on the issues. It just isn't practical for the CEO to have a junior officer make those decisions by which a corporation affects society."[3]

[2]Arjay Miller, cited in "The Chief Executive Officer," *Business Week,* May 4, 1974, p. 42.
[3]Cited in "The Chief Executive Officer," *Business Week,* May 4, 1974, *passim.*

Consensus Management in the Corporation

The search is on within the corporation for some form of divided responsibility or consensus management that will not lose effectiveness and efficiency. It is important to identify and sort out the personal talents that are required for dealing with both the internal and external affairs of the company, and to make certain those talents are both available and located in responsible and authoritative assignments.

One solution that has been used with increasing frequency to spread the responsibilities for *operating* matters is the device of the "Office of the Chief Executive." Here, the Office of the Chief Executive usually consists of from three to five senior officers of the company, including, of course, the chief executive officer himself. External affairs are often left to the chief executive officer, sometimes assisted by a public relations department and sometimes not. But a more logical and effective place to locate the talents, attitudes, and experience needed to relieve the chief executive officer and his executive associates of the load of *external* affairs is in a reconstituted board of directors with broad social as well as business interests.

The jobs of the chief executive officer and his executive associates, on the one hand, and of the chairman of the board and his director colleagues, on the other, are necessarily and irrevocably interrelated. Recognition of the primacy of their respective authorities, however, can help to assure that corporations will, in the future, demonstrate a responsiveness to public expectations that has not heretofore been experienced. The executive officers in management are properly the initiators in matters directly related to currently running the business, subject to review and audit by the board. The board members are properly the initiators of broad policies and programs to guide operations. In addition, they are the natural interpreters of the company to its several outside "publics" as well as the interpreters of the demands or positions of those "publics" to the executive officers of the company.

This distribution of initiating responsibility implies that boards should include members who are broadly read, have associations in numerous communities of the public, and possess a capability for oral and written expression, as well as an intimate knowledge of the business and the company. While all of this breadth of talent and background is not likely to be found in one individual, the composition of the board, if it has been carefully selected, could reasonably be expected to provide the company with the broadly based strengths that are required.

It must be recognized that a response to public expectations more frequently than not involves an immediate expense without a compensating addition to income. The maximization of short-term profits is necessarily modified by most actions related to social responsibility, even though long-range profit may be made more secure. In such situations, it is as important for management to check and balance board initiatives that represent a response to public purposes or pressures as it is for the board to review the operating proposals of management for consistency with approved policy. It is a merit of the combination of a strong board and a strong management that the resolutions of specific issues are likely to be the most rational and, in the long run, the most desirable.

A redefinition of the job of the chief executive officer can be articulated either by specifying what he and his executive associates should do or by determining what kinds of interests and decisions the board wishes to retain or recapture for itself. The latter may be the most instructive approach. With respect to purely business affairs, the board is essentially a policy and review body that delegates current operations to management. While it may be legally responsible for fixing policy and purpose, the board would be foolish to do so without the benefit of close collaboration and consultation with management. Great care must be taken to avoid participating—i.e., interfering—in operations after purposes and programs have been discussed and adopted. Operations must be left to management.

It is in the external relations of the company that the board should identify tasks for which it is uniquely qualified and take more initiative; otherwise confusion of responsibility is most likely to occur. Governmental agencies working in the fields of competition and monopoly, labor, and taxes are logical, primary external contacts for management. All other external contacts, including even those with stockholders, can probably be handled as effectively, perhaps more effectively, by a properly organized working board. In part, the resolution of the distribution of functions between the chief executive officer and the chairman of the board would depend on the personalities involved; but, other things being equal, it is better for the sound development of the organization to adjust personnel to a rational assignment of functions than to adjust the functions to the talents of those available. However, other things are seldom equal and change from existing patterns must be careful and deliberate. In the interest of continuity and stability, basic changes will no doubt occur in part through attrition and in part through deliberate action.

5

Organizing the Working Board

A closer look at the means for exercising some of the functions and responsibilities of directors proposed here will illustrate the subtle nuances involved in collaboration between the board and management. A clarification of the relationship between the board and management can be achieved most effectively by the development of active and substantive committees of the board. The development of a system of committees is facilitated by a prior identification and assignment, between the board and management, of initiating responsibility for specific proposals. The use of committees has the potential of making both the board and management more effective in their respective areas of primary interest.

There are six major areas concerning the *internal* operations of a company to which the board's attention must from time to time be focused. Management should have the initiating responsibility for these first three: (1) specific recommendations for the commitment of the company's resources, (2) the operating program for the year, or years, immediately ahead, together with analysis of its financial implications, and (3) proposals for administrative structures and procedures that are best adapted to the nature of the company, and for systems of internal reporting and communications for the purposes of audit and control. Management *or* the board, depending on circumstances, should have initiating responsibility for these three: (4) possible conflicts of interests within the company and between the company and outside interests. These may involve executives and members of the board as well as the staff; (5) the compensation, fringe benefits, and pension arrangements for both wage and salary personnel; and (6) last, but not least, assuring orderly personnel policies and competent management in depth, including arrangements for orderly succession at all senior levels.

The *external* concerns of a company include problems of the environment and conservation, community tensions resulting from discrimination and poverty, and the sociopolitical posture of the corporation in matters that reach beyond its conformity to the minimum requirements of law. Moreover, thoughtfully drafted external communications are required to assure that effective internal and external performance becomes widely known. For reasons that have been previously set forth in this book, initiating responsibility for the relationship of the company to the society outside the corporation can be most effectively lodged in the board, with management providing estimates of the costs of any contemplated actions.

In all of these matters, both inside and outside the organization, a tradition of mutually helpful collaboration between the board and management will be strong if based both on a clear identification of the respective initiating responsibilities and on the acceptance by each of the practice of initiation by the other.

There are probably as many ways to organize the work of a board of directors as there are boards. It would be difficult to find two that are exactly alike. Differences depend in part on the nature of the business, in part on company history and traditions, in part on dominant personalities. A system of committees is typical of most boards, but there are, no doubt, many boards that do not have committees at all. It has usually been found, however, to be an effective device for getting the board's work done; and there can be little doubt that this type of structure has the advantage of facilitating a positive collaboration between the board, the chief executive officer, and his executive associates. Without such a structure, there is at least the suggestion that the management team has little enthusiasm for an active and assertive collaboration.

Although the committee structure considered desirable or necessary will vary from company to company, among the committees that may be needed in larger corporations to cover the board's activities adequately are: (1) an executive committee, (2) a finance committee, (3) an audit and corporate organization committee, (4) a conflicts of interests and legal affairs committee, (5) a compensation and pension committee, and (6) a personnel, management development, and succession committee. Members of all these committees should be nominated by the chairman and confirmed by the whole board. The chairmen of these committees, just as the chairman of the board itself, should be officers of the board and not of the company.

There is, of course, nothing absolute about this assignment of tasks to particular committees of the board. Successful corporations like General Electric and General Motors have adopted quite different committee structures. For example, both have public policy committees, one calling it a public issues committee. They have the assignment to study major public issues and assess what the management's response to them should be in its posture, policies, programs, and practices. In our view, this is a task for the whole board; and it is the task of each of the board's committees to appraise the activity of its particular interest in the light of broad social as well as economic values. Still other committee patterns also appear in current practice. Thus, high technology companies may include a science advancement committee or a technology and science committee in their roster of board committees.

A defensible variation from the pattern suggested above might combine the compensation and pension committee with the personnel, management development, and succession committee on the premise that management development functionally involves everything that has to do with people and their incentives. Another variation might combine the conflicts of interests committee with the audit committee. Indeed, medium-sized and smaller companies would no doubt find both fewer committees and different combinations of assignments more effective in serving their needs.

Several additional observations of a general nature should be made before discussing the particular committees. Board committees should be established by the whole board only after a review and discussion of a previously prepared set of assignments and duties. In other words, each committee should have a written charter, subject to modification or withdrawal by the whole board, when and if circumstances change. For maximum effectiveness, membership on committees should be small, usually no more than three or four; and the chairman of each committee should be a member of the board who is not an officer of the company. There is no reason why the chairman of the board, if his time permits, might not serve also as chairman of one or more committees. The issue of rotating committee membership can only be decided after an examination of the particular circumstances and personalities. When they are needed, the chief executive officer and his executive associates should make members of the company staff available to committees of the board. The frequency, or the degree of regularity or irregularity, of committee meetings, must, of course, depend on the extent of the tasks to be accomplished.

Finally, a word should be said about the possibility of a committee, secured by its charter, becoming a maverick among its fellow board members and the company's executive management. While such a development is a possibility, it is hardly a probability as long as committee membership is limited to a minority of the board; in the extreme, its charter, given by the full board, can be rescinded by board action. But board members are generally rational people and so drastic a remedy is not likely to be required.

Without attempting to prescribe a committee structure that would serve a particular company best, it may be useful to describe a pattern that will further illustrate the range of interests of the full board and present some of the nuances involved in close board collaboration with the chief executive officer and his executive associates.

The Executive Committee

The commitment of a company's resources provides an excellent illustration of the difference between the board functions of establishing policy and procedures, and reviewing performance, on the one hand, and the management execution of an operating program that gives expression to such policy and procedures, on the other hand.

66

Even though many corporations are identified with a specific area of activity, in fact, most corporations have assets in several areas, and these are usually in a continuous state of flux. They must be renewed or changed as they deplete or depreciate. Peripheral activities may become more attractive. Foreign investments compete with domestic. In an age of conglomeration, entirely new types of activity may be acquired. Trade practice legislation may encourage vertical integration and discourage horizontal integration, or vice versa, or discourage both. Certain investment areas may reach substantial saturation, others a diminishing rate of growth, still others a take-off threshold for dynamic growth. Patents are granted and expire. Research and development activities by government, by the company, and by others also influence decisions to expand or withdraw investment capital.

Put simply, a company must know where it wants to go in today's kaleidoscopic world and should be wary of coming upon the surprise realization that it is on a dead-end street. This becomes a real hazard when management submits proposals to invest or to withdraw capital on a schedule unrelated to a previously delineated, broad investment program. Experience has confirmed the inadequacy of this approach, even though each new proposal, in terms of its projected sales, costs, and profits, may appear to be attractive at the time of its presentation to the board for approval.

As opposed to this piecemeal approach, greater consistency and coordination can be achieved if the formulation of investment policy is made the responsibility of an executive committee of the board which presents its long-range program proposals for annual review and approval by the entire board. The chief executive officer should be a member, but not the chairman, of the executive committee, thus assuring the availability of manage-

ment's intimate knowledge and experience in policy formulation. Specific investment proposals for plant and
market expansion or product extension that fall within
the adopted policy should then have the "clear sailing" of
full board approval.

Those proposals that fall outside a previously approved
program and budget would be identified and judged on
their unique merits. It is desirable to have the executive
committee review all specific investment and divestment
proposals before they are presented to the full board; the
same is true of mergers and acquisitions.

A periodic review by the board—no less frequent than
once a year—of investments previously made should be
regularized to the point of being routine. The initiative
for specific proposals for action relating to investment and
disinvestment, however, belongs to management.

In all of these matters related to capital budgets, the
board members' interest is in appraising the compatibil-
ity of specific proposals with predetermined policy and
procedures, and in reviewing performance against the
expectations with which the investments were made. A
convenient means of giving expression to policy formulation is through the periodic discussion, modification, and
approval of a five-year development program and the
operating expectations that accompany it. Such a program, of course, constitutes a moving target that continuously changes its contours and dimensions, even at
times its direction. This procedure provides a better grasp
of the company's future than can be achieved through
more generalized expressions of purpose and strategy.

The chairman of the executive committee should, if
possible, have been a successful career officer in the
company or in the major field, or fields, of its activities;
but he, like the chairman of the board, should now be an
officer of the board and no longer an officer of the com-

pany. Depending upon the particular circumstances, it may be desirable that the chairman of the board serve also as chairman of the executive committee.

The Finance Committee

Companies have different traditions. Although an overview of the capital budget is, logically, a primary task of the executive committee, the preliminary review of the *operating* budget and its financing for the year ahead may or may not be. In most cases the operations budget would be more appropriately assigned to the finance committee for review and analysis of its implications for the prospective flow of total receipts and disbursements, after it has been prepared by company staff under management's supervision. Then it would go to the full board for review and approval, after which it would serve as a bench mark to measure operations periodically during the year.

Financial planning and control is the major device used to assure a balanced and effective operating program. Based on the board's policy consensus, the operating budget would originate with strategic decisions at the executive level of management, then fan out to the tactical planning of middle management. The program would then be further developed by operating managers. Financial expression is the measure used throughout the process; additionally, projections of operating data support the monetary estimates.

Assumptions based on past markets and future price expectations are related to anticipated costs and used to project cash flows and financing needs. The prospective performance of inventories and the behavior of receivables are major considerations in the analysis as are the inflationary pressures in the economy and the cost of money. The least predictable factor, however, is the future level of total activity in the company's field of business, which is, of course, a function of the general business cycle. All the mature judgment that is available should be enlisted for the analysis, including that of competently trained economists.

The initiating work in strategic and tactical planning is done by management, but consultation with an informed finance committee of the board and periodic review by the entire board can bring to a company's financial management an added dimension of experience and knowledge. Moreover, intimate knowledge of the money and securities markets and associations with the financial community can facilitate both the short-term and the long-term external financing that may be needed.

Another major concern of the finance committee should be assuring and maintaining financial credibility among investors and the public at large. The federal government and the organized securities markets have tightened their rules of disclosure, but a skeptical public, which has observed too many horror stories of mismanagement or outright deceit in recent years, remains unconvinced. But beyond the legal requirements for disclosure, the board must fulfill the informational requirements of the company's several publics: the financial community, the news media, government agencies, and, last but not least, the stockholders. The finance committee, if it is made responsible for initial review of the operating budget, is the natural locus of ultimate responsibility for the integrity of the company's financial reporting to the public. The chairman of the whole board may be the most frequent spokesman for the company, but he needs the careful work of his fellow finance committee members, who follow the company's operating program closely.

The Audit and Corporate Organization Committee

Financial planning and the audit of a company's performance have a close affinity and in many companies they are combined in a single board committee. There is something to be said for these functions being handled by separate committees, however, if the resources and talents are available among the board members. As set forth in the preceding section, the finance committee would focus for the most part, but not exclusively, on current operations, the expectations for the year or so ahead, and the provision of the financial requirements to support the approved program of the company. The audit committee, on the other hand, supervises management's compilation and maintenance of accurate and current records, as well as the procedures for reporting results of operations and the identification of malfeasance.

A communications system must be developed to report both financial and operating data in a form to give it analytical and operating significance. It is a highly complicated task of management to design an effective system of internal communications, but such is essential to provide the data for orderly management and cost control. An adequate system must make all relevant information, *both good and bad,* available to both management and the board. It is at this point that the present practices of many boards have been most vulnerable to criticism. Prompt disclosure to the board of malfeasance or bad judgment must be certain.

An effective system of communications should enable board members to appraise the total operation as well as its parts. The system itself would be devised by management but board review of the procedures incorporated in it is necessary to establish confidence on the part of all those involved, including the public. The development of the channels for the flow of financial and operating

71

data for management control and board guidance must fit integrally into the total corporate structure. This has been recognized by most of the leading accounting firms in the development of their management consulting divisions in recent years. In its periodic conferences with outside auditors, the audit and corporate organization committee should satisfy itself that the company's accounts are accurate and comprehensive, that the communications system by which they were gathered is adequate, and that the data are reported on the basis of commonly accepted accounting principles.

In addition to the supervision of auditing procedures, this committee must keep a constant eye on the company's organization. Different businesses require different administrative structures, and the most appropriate structure for a particular company may differ with the passage of time. Periodic review of the organization structure, conducted jointly by management, a committee of the board, and perhaps outside consultants, can help to avoid rigidity at a time when both production technology and administrative capabilities, as well as the external environment, are changing very rapidly.

The traditional departmental structure may require significant modification and supplementation from time to time to adapt to new and unfamiliar tasks as well as to the global spread of business. The most difficult task ahead will be the administrative adjustments that will be needed to cope with the emerging commitment to help solve social and cultural problems. If the corporation is to be effective in extending its activities into this new and strange world, responsibilities must be assigned in a manner that is unfamiliar and new techniques for monitoring and auditing corporate performance in this novel area must be developed.

At regular intervals, this committee should review the administrative structure of the organization in the light of approved policies and the tasks to be accomplished. It would be especially appropriate for this committee to meet with outside management consultants, as well as with outside auditors, if the need for objective judgment is desired.

The Conflicts of Interests and Legal Affairs Committee

Conflicts of interests, potential or real, of board members, officers, and other employees raise issues that are often difficult and resist precise delineation. They may involve ethical as well as legal questions. They should be under continuous review by a committee of the board, but the establishment of a formal corporate policy requires careful thought. The development of procedures for monitoring conflicts of interests, often involving board resolutions, employee questionnaires and surveys, including the determination of their coverage and frequency of use, is no easier. Finally, methods of review and enforcement must be established.

Potential conflicts of interests characterize every phase of contemporary society. They are by no means limited to business situations. Examples from the world of politics appear daily in the public press. But the business community, like Caesar's wife, is judged by severe standards, and every effort must be made to minimize the opportunity to use an advantageous situation for personal gain at the expense of others.

There have been too many instances in recent years in which managements have sought profit at the expense of stockholders. Managers typically are heavily burdened people and should be provided with emoluments of various kinds to ease the physical and emotional demands of their daily schedules. But attempts at personal profit through the use of the resources of the company they are supposed to serve, in transactions that directly or indirectly result in personal gain without benefit to the company, are matters that boards of directors must police with great care and determination.

The disclosure of trade secrets or industrial spying are clear cases of conflicts of interests. Use of company credit directly or indirectly to support an external interest is another. The issues become more difficult to judge in a case where a director or a manager has an interest in a supplier that is able to provide better and more certain deliveries at competitive prices, or in the case where a company director serves on the board of a highly qualified and competitive investment banking house that has been awarded exclusive financing arrangements.

On the other hand, joint membership on boards of companies whose markets may overlap to a modest degree, so-called interlocking directorates, have only a limited potential for conflicts of interests. This matter has, nonetheless, been a major concern of the Federal Trade Commission in recent years. Several resignations have been decreed, based on the Clayton Act, but it is unclear that the actions will, in any discernible manner, influence competitive relations or practices among the companies involved. In the first place, the judicial "rule of reason" is so well known that it can be counted on to guide an honest management in negotiating the terms of a transaction. In the second place, management negotiates the typical transactions and not the directors.

Other potential areas of conflict result from the "moonlighting" of company personnel, or the transfer of talents, trade, and technological secrets in changing jobs. All energetic people in the course of time develop outside interests. Indeed, it is often to the benefit of the company that they do so. In recent years, the practice has grown of encouraging company personnel to participate in a wide variety of community and political affairs. These activi-

74

ties are completely appropriate. On the other hand, the disclosure of production and trade secrets, or the indirect facilitation of "industrial spying," are clearly cases of conflicts of interests. In between lie situations in which an outside activity may increase competition for the employee's company or may make a direct or indirect contribution to the financial strength of a competitor. Each case must be judged on its own terms. Using access to company information or resources for personal gain, the acceptance of excessive gifts or entertainment, the lack of uniformity in methods of purchasing, and outside employment that diminishes usefulness and efficiency for the company are the areas in which conflicts of interests are most likely to arise and hardest to measure.

Care must be taken in developing procedures to deal with conflicts of interests to avoid an undesirable restraint on the initiative of the officer or employee or on the morale of the organization. Opportunities for self-disclosure should be provided. Without intelligent application, monitoring of the activities of company personnel can become expensive without being effective in identifying the significant situations. However, the relevant activities of everyone in the organization, particularly those of the key officers whose activities are of crucial importance to the company, should be subject to the monitoring procedures. This includes all members of the board from the chairman down.

The many legal, social, ethical, and economic aspects of real and potential conflicts of interests make them a matter of major interest to a board of directors in its function of safeguarding the company's assets. It might be thought that the functions of the conflicts of interests committee might be more appropriately combined with the committee on audit. These two committees must obviously work closely together, but to combine them could have the disadvantage of placing too great an emphasis on the disclosure of mischief. This could sacrifice the full opportunity of the audit and corporate organization committee to share in the development of a communications system and administrative structure on the positive side of the company's operations.

The committee on conflicts of interests and legal affairs must necessarily maintain a close working relationship with both house and outside counsel. Through the committee, the full board should be fully informed regarding the legal aspects of mergers, the rulings of federal, state, and local regulatory agencies, and the limitations and restraints of all kinds that affect the company's operations. Of particular interest at the present are the tightening requirements for disclosure and the accompanying increase in the exposure of directors to personal liability.

Looking ahead, the legal tangles that may be encountered in the discharge of corporate social responsibility are just beginning to be apprehended. Robert L. Werner, General Counsel of RCA put it this way at a Conference Board meeting in 1974:

> What formerly may have involved only moral responsibility is now being translated into expanding legal responsibility imposed by a constantly growing body of new rules of law, new regulation, and new interpretations of existing law and regulation. . . .
> But, as in antitrust, when he endeavors to carry out his social responsibilities, the businessman can find himself confronted by a thicket of legal ambiguities, conflicting demands and jurisdictions. . . .[1]

The increasing exposure of directors to personal liability stemming from judicial rulings in cases involving the securities disclosure laws and to actions that are taken or

[1]Robert L. Werner, "Antitrust, Social Responsibility and Changing Times," *Antitrust and Shifting National Controls Policies: Impact on Differently Positioned Companies,* transcript of the Thirteenth Conference on Antitrust Issues in Today's Economy (New York: The Conference Board, Inc., 1974), p. 5.

not taken by management makes the work of the committee on conflicts of interests and legal affairs of major concern to the entire board. As Professor Lawrence Stessin put it in describing board membership in a *New York Times* article:

> What was once considered to be a badge of honor . . . has turned into a sensitive post that calls for hard work, sharp questions, an alert mind and a risk of one day looking down the barrel of a law suit filed by stockholders or social activists.[2]

A suggestion has been made that in addition to having access to the in-house and outside company counsel, this committee might have its own outside attorney to brief it on agenda matters just before committee or full board meetings. This briefing could constitute a kind of "preventive law," with each item on the agenda being reviewed from the standpoint of potential director's liability. But there are problems with this proposal, chief of which would be the danger that excessive caution would inhibit effective and prompt company action.

The Compensation and Pension Committee

Compensation, fringe benefits, perquisites and pension arrangements, particularly among senior executive officers of an organization, are matters that necessarily require review and decisions by the board. It is as important that base executive salary scales be fully competitive as it is that they be within reasonable bounds. Pension and other security arrangements, fringe benefits and salary ranges throughout the company should be reviewed by the full board after determination of their appropriateness by this committee.

[2]*New York Times*, May 26, 1974.

The most valuable resource possessed by an organization is the quality of its personnel, even though it is an asset that never appears on the balance sheet. Compensation and pension arrangements must be adequate to attract and retain effective people in a competitive market that seems never to be oversupplied. Part of the task of attracting and retaining highly qualified people is to provide working conditions that induce enthusiasm and loyalty. This is a subtle matter and cannot be bought with emoluments alone; but the provision to executive personnel of convenient cars with drivers for company business, clean and comfortable company operated accommodations in frequently visited non-home locations, company planes that save valuable time and avoid travel frustrations may all be appropriate devices to make the executive's life less hectic. Expense accounts for company related activities are a competitive must.

Pension plans along with other forms of compensation should also receive the careful attention of this committee for later review by the whole board of directors. These plans have wide variability. Deferred compensation arrangements may or may not influence the particular form of pensions provided. Some pensions are payable in company stock, some in lump sums of cash, some over the period of one or two lives; some provide for the spouse, some do not. Some pension plans are fully funded, some partially, and perhaps there are still some with no funding at all. The Pension Reform Act of 1974 requires that pension obligations be funded for existing plans after thirty years and for new plans after forty years. Vesting requirements under the new law will create additional problems.

Investments supporting the funding of pensions may be those of an insurance company, may be managed by a bank and held in its vault, commingled or separately identified; and, finally, the amount to which the pension liability is funded will depend upon actuarial assumptions, the assumed rate of interest, the investment management success, and the annual contributions of the company and/or participants. These are all matters that are developed as an overall program by management, after which they become a major responsibility for board review. Large amounts of money are involved. Generally, the performance of investment management of pension funds in recent years has not been impressive.

The determination of competitive salary scales has been facilitated in recent years by comparative industry studies prepared by management consulting firms with a specialty in this field and by the collection and correlation of salary data by industry associations. Even here, however, a variety of patterns results from different uses of deferred compensation, qualified and non-qualified stock options, and the awarding of shares based on performance in achieving predetermined company goals. Further, some companies have executive incentive compensation plans under which annual rewards depend upon a continuous improvement of earnings over a trailing base average. The board through its committee on compensation and pensions will wish to follow all of these matters closely to fulfill its responsibility for maintaining the company as an attractive place to work and as an organization fully capable of meeting its future pension liabilities.

Another matter of compensation concern must rest with the board simply because there is no other appropriate place to put it, namely, the compensation of board members themselves. This determination is, in most cases, now made by the chief executive officer, but that is simply another inversion of authority among the several noted in Chapter 2. Although numerous writers have held that board members are now underpaid, that is a conclusion that could only rest on the large risks to which they are exposed—not on the amount of work they typically do as boards are now organized and function.

To the extent that boards of directors reorganize themselves and function in a manner consistent with their basic authority and responsibilities—and only to that extent—the financial rewards of service should be, in most cases, much higher than at the present. In fact, it would be appropriate if board members' compensation reached the ratable equivalency of the senior executive officers of the company. This means that the chairman of the board, if indeed he spends as much time, thought, and effort as the chief executive officer, should be equally compensated. If the chairmen of the more important committees of the board put in 10, 20, or 30 percent of the time, thought, and effort of an executive vice president, they should be rewarded on the basis of ratable equivalency: 10, 20, or 30 percent of the company officer's full-time compensation. The compensation of other members of the board would be correspondingly adjusted depending upon their contribution. It is as important for the board to maintain the quality of its own membership through appropriate incentives as it is to maintain the effectiveness and capacity of executive management. The compensation of each board member should be reviewed annually, and recommendations by the committee on compensation and pensions for changes should go to the full board for its official approval.

The Personnel, Management Development, and Succession Committee

Policies and procedures to govern personnel practices fall conveniently into three categories: (1) employees under union contracts, if any, (2) other employees below junior management level, and (3) managers from junior grade through the chief executive officer. The board's interest should be mainly in the third category, less in the second, still less in the first. The development of effective personnel policies at all levels must be recognized, however, as a critically important element of a successful enterprise. The assurance of a "filled pipeline" of competent people is an absolute essential for the healthy, long-term future of the corporation. The committee of the board on personnel in its various aspects should have this as its overriding concern.

The disadvantages of board intervention in management's relations with unionized employees would far outweigh any advantages. Relations with unions would become very confused if more than one representation of the company were involved. There have been instances in recent years of boards of directors making "surprise audits" of personnel morale in troubled plants or where programs of affirmative action on behalf of minorities have not been convincingly fulfilled. By and large these are matters of initial concern to management, however, and excessive involvement in them by the board could set awkward precedents available for abuse by the aggrieved. It is well to remember that the board's task is basically to determine personnel policies and procedures, and to make certain that they are well known and understood, that they have provisions for on-the-job safety, that they are reasonably stable, and that no opportunities to improve job satisfaction and to increase productivity are overlooked. Part of that task is, of course, to insure that wages and salaries, including fringes, whether or not on a contract, are competitive. But negotiations with organized labor are management's job.

It is in the third category of employees, which includes managers at the lowest grade through and including the chief executive officer, where the board's involvement must be the greatest, especially in the higher grades. In addition to salary, there are numerous other aspects of the employment of managers, such as job rotation, frequency of family movement, housing facilitation, and travel, in which the committee on personnel must take an interest even though the specific decisions rest with management. All of these considerations relate directly or indirectly to the development of the individual as a maturing manager.

The committee on personnel, management development, and succession will want to review the full range of activities related to the identification and training of managers. A practice that has grown in recent years is the executive training program, which may be conducted "in house" or on a university campus. These are scheduled for varying periods of time. The manager is released from daily duties for a period of study and discussion. This is a practice developed earlier by the military and by other professions such as medicine and engineering.

The committee will also want to be familiar with the more important changes in executive assignment. The chief executive officer should make such assignments as a matter of personal preference and accommodation toward the end of developing a harmonious team of officers. While he will wish to discuss his plans for management personnel with the committee, there should be no implication of a veto power by the committee except in extraordinary circumstances.

The most sensitive, but also the most critical, function of a committee on personnel, management development, and succession is to assure an orderly transition when the chief executive officer, for whatever reason, vacates his position. The quality and characteristics of most organizations are a projection of the individual who leads them. When a new leader is chosen, styles of operating change and a certain quality and continuity of ideas is broken; but if perceptive care is exercised, the most successful features of the past can be carried forward into the future. The leader here is the chief executive officer, and his successor should be chosen through an objective and formalized screening process with plenty of lead time, which is usually available except in the case of catastrophe. The recommendations of the committee charged with picking a successor chief executive officer should be submitted to the entire board and rigorously and impersonally appraised. While the views of the present chief executive officer should, of course, be sought, the task of choosing his successor should not be handed to or imposed on him; it is bound to be a selection in which he is too personally and emotionally involved.

Another task of succession is the replenishment of the board itself. It is generally true that entry into and exit from board membership today is informal and, apart from retirement because of age, mainly dependent on the judgment and desire of the chief executive officer rather than on the ownership of stock or on more than formal approval by the stockholders. In these circumstances, the influence of the chief executive officer on a board member's sense of independence, or lack thereof, is self-evident.

It should be a primary concern of the board to keep its own membership refreshed and effective. Its members should feel a sense of commitment and dedication without the hazard of retribution if they take positions that do not coincide with those of the chairman, or, with those of the chief executive officer. That is now a difficult stance for a board member to take in the light of present informal procedures for entry into and exit from a board of directors. A screening procedure for both the entry and exit of board members, administered by a committee of the board on personnel, management development, and succession, could contribute constructively to objective policy determination. Procedures for the recruitment and termination of board members should be developed and be widely understood.

Working Committees Make a Working Board

All of the foregoing activities proposed for the several committees of the board fall outside of the day-to-day transactions and operations of the company's procurement, production, transportation, and marketing. These activities are now typically performed by someone in the company, usually in the middle management, reviewed by the senior management, and then reported to the board. The report is usually brief and is mainly background for the management's recommendations. The elaborate analysis that precedes the recommendations and the other opinions developed in the analytical process are not usually available for the board's review. This, in fact, is a process of decision making that limits the usefulness of the experience and insight of board members and exposes the board as a whole to allegations of neglect.

The extent to which the members of the several committees of the board become involved in the processes of analysis in the respective fields of their committee assignments, prior to a report to the whole board, is a matter that would vary with company traditions, the nature of the particular problem, and the personalities involved. But a gradual increase in involvement by board members through their committees could be beneficial in numerous ways. It would add a dimension of mature judgment during the process of analysis and appraisal that would otherwise be unavailable. It would assure a comprehensive discussion at the full board meeting of both the positive—and the negative—aspects of a given issue. It would help board members become familiar with management personnel in the junior and middle, as well as the senior, grades. Finally, *it would establish a record of participation and supervision that would be hard for critics of the corporation and its procedures to challenge.*

The failure of a company to develop an effective committee structure for the positive work of the board means running the risk of having such a structure imposed by outside interests as evidenced by the judgment in the recent Securities and Exchange Commission v. Mattel case. Confronted with false documentation and financial difficulties the court took drastic action. It took and retained jurisdiction of the company "in order to implement and carry out the terms of its decree and of all additional decrees or orders that may be appropriate. . . ." It ordered Mattel, within sixty days, to appoint enough additional directors to constitute a majority of the board. It was decreed that these new directors be satisfactory to the SEC as well as to Mattel, and that they be approved by the court prior to their assumption of board membership.

An executive committee of not less than three was decreed, a majority of whom would be newly appointed and approved members of the board. The court further ordered the establishment of a financial controls and audit committee, with not less than three of its four members to come from the newly appointed board members. The functions of this committee were described in some detail in the court's order. A litigation and claims committee of three newly appointed directors was ordered to examine past, present, and future conflicts of interests. Finally, the new directors were ordered to appoint a special counsel to represent them in their investigation of the company's affairs, and he, in turn, was required to appoint a special auditor to help in this investigation. It is true that the accounts of Mattel contained numerous doubtful entries that would not be present in well-managed companies; but the point is that the failure by the board to take positive action to organize itself and to assure that it was adequately informed exposed the company and the board to a court imposed and supervised operation.

It should be recognized that greater participation and involvement through the development of an adequate committee structure of a board would require the commitment of much more time and hard work by board members than is now typical. It is to an exploration of the feasibility of finding talent qualified to man the working board that we now turn.

6

The Composition of the Board

THE former Chairman of the Securities and Exchange Commission, Ray D. Garrett, Jr., has recently observed:

> Possibly, we should endorse one or more of the suggestions recently made by proponents of reform in the boardroom and intended to enhance the abilities of outside directors adequately to meet their responsibilities, such as the use of full-time, full-salaried outside directors.[1]

Most corporations, however, do not currently have a sufficient supply of talented executives to fill both their top management and full-time board positions. Nor is it possible at present to identify outside a company adequate numbers of qualified individuals committed to full-time service on one or more boards. Where can directors capable of greater or full-time commitments, and with the required qualifications, be found? Talent and capability in combination with a sense of commitment are not easy to come by.

Before the type of working board described in earlier pages could be expected to develop on a broad scale, an

[1]Ray D. Garrett, Jr., "The SEC Study of Directors' Guidelines," *The Conference Board RECORD*, July, 1974.

additional number of hard questions should be considered:

1. Is it realistic to expect all board members, other than the chief executive officer, to discontinue functioning as officers of the company? Should all company officers except the chief executive officer be relieved of operational responsibilities on joining the board?

2. How many members should a board have? What criteria should be used in determining the size of a board?

3. What are the most likely sources of board members not previously associated with the company?

4. How can the supply of people qualified for board work be increased? Can it be? How much time should board members commit to their work?

5. Can the addition of directors who represent special interests be expected to increase the supply of qualified persons? Is it desirable to elect such directors?

6. Can challenges in addition to improved compensation make board membership more attractive?

7. What kind of perquisites, in addition to compensation, are appropriate for board members? What accommodations or other facilities should be made available, if any? Where located?

8. What is the most likely source of a chairman of the board?

There are probably as many ways to answer most of these questions as there are corporations. It is possible, however, to provide some general observations.

The Supply of Competent Directors

Most of our discussion has suggested that the supply of qualified directors is limited. Numerous considerations necessarily enter into an effort to estimate the total current supply of, and demand for, qualified directors. The supply of those qualified under the conditions and circumstances proposed here for the "working board" would indeed be inadequate if the transition from present practices should occur rapidly and in a large number of corporations at the same time. There is, however, little prospect of this happening; nor would it be desirable that the work patterns of boards be changed too quickly. A process of trial and error, a testing of a general direction of change, would be more appropriate.

One point should be made with emphasis, however. The size of the pool of those both capable and available is inelastic only for relatively short periods. It is flexible and would expand over reasonable periods of time as the attractiveness of board membership increased. Financial rewards would be only one element of that attractiveness. Probably more important would be the opportunity and challenge to make a significant contribution, to feel a part of a group whose decisions have ultimate meaning in the governance of the enterprise. The attractiveness of board membership would also increase if exposure to presently unclear and unidentified legal liabilities were reduced.

Although the idea of a "professional director" has gained some favor in recent years, it is probably premature to envisage the rapid emergence of a pool of qualified, professional board talent before the role and legal exposure of directors is further clarified. Robert M. Estes of General Electric has put it succinctly:

> The profession has no formal entrance requirements; no precise standards for measuring performance; no self-policing apparatus; the finest of its members are highly skilled, underpaid, and overworked; they are vulnerable to betrayal by a venal minority and a cynical, uninformed public; and they are subjected to a wide range of legal assaults.[2]

[2]Robert M. Estes, "Liability and the Director," *The Board of Directors: New Challenges, New Directions,* A Conference Report from the

Yet is is no doubt true that, if the attractiveness of board membership were enhanced, many highly competent people would seriously consider second careers as professional directors after early retirement from a variety of first career experiences. Those who contemplated future careers as directors, knowing that such service would require a breadth of vision, interest, and understanding beyond the confines of daily operating assignments, would be encouraged, during their first career, to extend their knowledge, reading, experiences, and contacts to a variety of fields.

The possibility of a second career, involving a release from routine activities, the prospect of living with intellectually exhilarating challenges, and an opportunity to share in constructive leadership, would serve as a powerful magnet to attract experienced and talented people and, in time, enlarge the pool of those eligible for board positions in the future. The now visible trend toward an earlier retirement from daily operating responsibilities is already enlarging the number of competent and proven executives who can be called upon in selected cases, to the benefit of both the individual and the activity with which he or she joins. The International Executive Service Corps provides an interesting example of capabilities that have been rededicated after retirement.

The Supply of Director-time

The supply of directors is one thing; the supply of director-time is quite another. A greater participation in the

---

Conference Board, November 18, 1971 (New York: The Conference Board, 1972), p. 12.

determination of policy, procedures, personnel matters and the review of performance implies the commitment of more time and attention than is the present practice of most directors. But even to analyze the amount of time currently spent on board activities, per se, would be difficult. First, under the current general arrangements, with strong inside director participation on the board, most board work is reduced to an aspect of the operating duties of the officers of the company. Outside directors, for the most part, spend only a few hours each month and perhaps an additional four or five days a year on board business. Many of these are members of a number of boards and divide their available time among them.

Under the proposals being made here, the extent of the assignment and performance of board work will vary among the directors, some of whom will previously have been operating officers of the company. It is probable that adequate board work for some members will require as much as a third of a normal working schedule, and some members of the board, such as the chairman, may work full-time or even overtime on the work of the board.

At present, it is often the case that an individual with high visibility, particularly someone from the financial community, will serve on as many as ten, twenty, or even more boards. This can only mean infrequent attendance at meetings, limited familiarity with the company, and the ability to serve fully only at a time of crisis. In contrast, a member of a "working board" would find that his duties would preclude membership on more than a couple of boards and their committees. If he happens also to be the chief executive officer or chairman of the board of a company of some size, he probably would not wish to accept membership on more than one working board. Indeed, it is not uncommon now for companies to permit their top officers membership on only one outside board.

The Size of Boards

Related to the issue of the amount of time directors should spend on board work is the matter of the size of boards. On many present boards, composed largely of managers, some four to six members are active as participants, and perhaps ten to fifteen are fairly passive, reluctant to express a point of view unless it is solicited. This is a way of observing that, probably, most boards are too large as they now function.

Whether a "working board" of fifteen or twenty would be too large is a matter that could be determined by the tasks performed and by experience. The six committees described in Chapter 5, each with three or four members, with no overlaps, would mean a board of eighteen to twenty-four, plus the chairman of the board. There is no reason, however, to try to avoid overlap; indeed, overlap of certain committee assignments has definite advantages, if a board member devotes adequate time to each committee on which he serves. Through overlap and perhaps through combining some of the committees described, the total size of the board could be significantly reduced.

Other Sources and Non-Sources of Directors

The more traditional, tried, and tested sources of directorship talent have been corporate officers, both active and retired, lawyers, and investment and commercial bankers. In recent years, however, some new sources have been tried. The practice has grown of adding to boards academics—frequently administrators—women, representatives of minorities such as blacks, and, in rare instances, youth. Of late, proposals have been made with increasing frequency to add government representatives to corporate boards. Representation from consumers and labor also have their advocates. Demands are even heard that that amorphous constituency, "the public," be represented.

Special group representation on boards has been much debated and, to a degree, has been accepted. The argument has been made that all the major groups in society that are affected by a corporation should have representation on its board and that it is actually to the advantage of a corporation to have firsthand access to representatives of the major currents of contemporary society. Indeed, public pressure for greater independence in board members seems to have been the influence that has led some companies to accept the notion of the specialized representation of groups such as women, ethnic minorities, consumers, *et al.*

But it is not clear how the interests of multiple, sometimes political, and even opposing constituencies can, in the long run, be reconciled with the best interests of the company as basically an economic institution. Granted that the public's sanction of the corporation as an economic entity depends ultimately upon the approval of the other interest groups in the community, it is still not called upon to become a legislative assembly. In its own interests, it should be more concerned with the general community than it has been, but the corporation cannot be effective if it becomes quasi-political.

No doubt some of the demands for interest group representation stem from a certain lethargy among many boards of directors in dealing with the social and moral aspects of their corporate activities. There is a reluctance to challenge established positions and practices or to respond to changing expectations and the adoption of different values in our dynamic contemporary society. Unless, under the chairman's encouragement, a spirit and tradition of facing up to these problems can be activated among board members, it may be desirable and necessary to add interest group representatives to serve for a period as "catfish in the herring tank." In the long run, however, a board consisting predominantly of members serving specialized interests could not be expected to maximize the development of the total enterprise.

Effective specialized representation by its nature would result in political conflict on the board and make action in the general interest more difficult. Indeed, effective service to a particular group may constitute a conflict of interests with the institution a board member is elected to help govern. Over time, all the interests of the separate parties directly or indirectly affected by the enterprise will be best served by its balanced and healthy total development. The chairman of the board can do much to provide that unifying influence.

This is not to say that specialized interests should go unsponsored. With an appropriate degree of independence, all members of the board could be expected to espouse special causes from time to time, and not just the causes of their own socioeconomic group. All who are worthy of board membership should do this, regardless of their sex, race, religion, or ethnic background. The intelligence, knowledge, and character of the director should be paramount in board work. And it is the task of the chairman to encourage the free expression of those qualities in the interest of the total enterprise. Positive encouragement of such qualities by a chairman can provide better solutions to the problems confronting the company than the device of selecting directors simply because they represent a particular constituency.

The notion of selecting members of the board to represent consumers, the community at large, or the "public" seems even less promising. A basic difficulty, of course, is the matter of selection. Everyone is a consumer and a member of the public. The consumer and public community can become very large indeed in the case of the corporation whose activities cover the nation or the world. In this connection, it is interesting to note that the mutual insurance companies and savings institutions have boards that represent primarily the consumers of their services, but little difference has been noted between the attitudes or characteristic performance of their trustees and the boards of directors of stock companies.

The growing practice of having one or more foreign representatives on the boards of multinational corporations is the most promising of the special interest proposals. This is not because of unique or special attitudes and talents brought to the board so much as because multinational participation may mitigate somewhat the sharp penalties imposed on the global company by excessive chauvinism. There can also be a significant value in having on the board a perceptive interpreter of the different cultural traditions and commercial practices of other nations.

Co-determination: A Form of Labor Representation

Another special interest proposal is that employees be represented on corporate boards. This proposal has had increasing acceptance in Western Europe, particularly in Holland, Sweden, Norway, France, and Germany. The conspicuous case has been Germany, where "co-determination" has had an extended and not too successful experience. Co-determination is based on the assumption that business organizations should not be run solely by owners and/or managers; rather, the workers should also have a share in their administration. This is accomplished by a bifurcation of the unitary governing board into a supervisory council and a managing board. The supervisory council serves for a term of not more than four years. Some members are chosen by stockholders and some by workers; those chosen may not sit on the managing board. The managing board might be thought of as a rough equivalent to the president's or chairman's office now found in many management arrangements in the United States. The supervisory council and its practices are more like the contemporary board in the United States, but perhaps somewhat less effective.

The supervisory council appoints the top managers and has a veto on certain types of transactions, but otherwise is not expected to interfere with the management of the corporation's business. Meetings are typically scheduled on a quarterly basis. Labor representatives are on the council by force of law, but in combination with other special interest groups with perspectives and preoccupations of their own, effective evaluation and supervision of management is at best an indifferent matter. Some have felt that German corporations have been successful in their business operations despite co-determination, simply because the councils have been without major influence. It is premature to judge whether German corporations have been similarly successful in fulfilling public expectations of a societal nature. One might very well anticipate an outcome comparable to the German experience if board reform in the United States should take the direction of special interest representation without redefining and revitalizing the board's functions and practices.

Interest Group Directors Evaluated

One can logically ask, moreover, whether special interest directors, including labor representatives, would more likely be concerned than others with the impact of the corporation on the community at large. The assertion of the group self-interest of each specialized representative is the more probable. The result could be seriously debilitating to the corporation. In the opinion of Professor Phillip I. Blumberg, it

> . . . would transform the board into a political institution, a microcosm of the community. All the directors would become, in effect, special interest representatives (whether for an outside group or simply for the stockholders), working to satisfy their particular constituency. The problem of conflict of interest for the individual board members would be replaced by the problem of conflict among the directors. It is extremely doubtful that such a board could manage a corporation effectively. Board decisions would involve shifting alliances between constituent groups, with log rolling deals (for the exchange of support for respective proposals), all of which would lead to a condition described by Beardsley Ruml decades ago as "gangsterism."[3]

The present preoccupation with specialized representation on corporate boards may prove, in time, to be more a force that brings about recognition of the need for greater independence among all board members than an actual springboard for bringing very many representatives of special interest groups onto boards of directors. From the standpoint of the company, its operations, and relations to society, it is more important to have a rigorous and informed review of initiatives and proposals that reach the agenda than to have contending and specialized individuals on the board to represent limited constituencies.

Government Representatives

Still another proposal, one that has the plausibility of getting away from the infirmities of special interest representation but presumably could be expected to assure a hearing for the public interest, is to have appointments made to boards by the federal or state governments.

[3]Phillip I. Blumberg, "Who Belongs on Corporate Boards?," *Business & Society Review*, No. 5, Spring 1973, pp. 40–7.

These so-called public directors would be charged with the responsibility to represent the interests of all groups in society in their direct or indirect relationships to the corporation. Public directors, not being beholden to anyone other than government, might be expected, it is said, to exercise a degree of accountability and increased public sensitivity that could not otherwise be achieved.

There are precedents for the appointment of government directors to corporate boards, but the results seem to have been more neutral than positive. And, there is the difficult question of the selection of such directors. Who will do the selecting and how will it be done? There is no tradition to provide confidence that government officers are more capable than others in identifying and nominating capable people with a breadth of vision. To the contrary, there is a strong pressure in the political world to award the plums as recognition for past favors or to those most likely to reciprocate. Many have a justifiable lack of confidence in government and would have doubts about the kind of people that would be selected.

Finally, it is not at all certain that the representatives of government on boards of directors would have better insight with respect to policies and programs that would genuinely serve the public interest than would those with greater experience in corporate or other community affairs. The experiments that are now being made with boards composed of government and other representatives, such as the Communications Satellite Corporation and the prospective corporation to take over the reorganized northeastern railroads, have yet to yield firm evidence one way or another. An early experiment with the Union Pacific Railroad was inconclusive and subsequently discontinued. On the other hand, the appointment of one quarter of the directors of the Prudential Insurance Company by the Chief Justice of the New Jersey Supreme

Court does not seem to have impaired the effectiveness of its board.

The Potential of Non-Business Directors

At the present, only rarely have those representing blacks, women, government, etc., on boards of directors had significant business experience in their backgrounds. That does not necessarily destroy their usefulness as board members. If they are able to relate to the needs of the company and if their perception of external influences that will affect its future is sharp, they may make very important contributions. People with quite different backgrounds can bring a useful perspective to board deliberations, especially if they place the interests of the organization ahead of the specialized interests derived from those backgrounds.

Other non-business persons who have been added to boards with increasing frequency have been from the fields of education, usually academic administrators, and occasionally, the military, medicine, journalism, or professional writing, and, even more rarely, the ministry. Although it is not a good reason by itself, adding non-business people to boards can have a public relations value to a corporation. There is a widespread public skepticism of the ability of corporate management to understand the needs, or even be aware of the aspirations, of politically potent elements in society. Additions to the board from such groups may help to forestall mandated representation from such groups.

Accountants, Bankers, and Lawyers as Board Members

In general, the professions including accounting, but excepting the law, have not supplied a significant number of board members of business corporations, even after retirement. This is somewhat surprising in the case of accounting because the accountant, like the lawyer, spends his life career in close proximity to the world of business. It is, of course, understandable why immediate conflicts of interests would be involved if an accountant should serve on a board of directors while in actual professional practice, but after retirement his knowledge and experience could be very valuable to a board's deliberations.

Two traditional fields from which directors have been recruited are investment banking and commercial banking. There has been much debate as to whether the presence of an investment banker on the board results in a conflict of interests, or, more importantly, a restriction of the corporation's financing options. The same point has been made with respect to commercial bankers with significant trust departments, unless the banker refrains from buying and selling or advising with respect to the securities of the corporation on whose board he serves. More serious than conflicts of interests may be the limitation on the company's range of options in its financing activities, in its negotiation of loan arrangements, and in its public financing in the securities markets. Too often the company's business is limited to the bank or investment house represented on its board. Some companies, however, have added investment and commercial bankers to their boards accompanied by a policy of nonpreferential relationship to the financial institutions represented.

If the difficulties of conflicts of interests and limitation of financing options can be circumvented, investment bankers can make valuable additions to a board of directors. Witness Gustave L. Levy, Senior Partner of Goldman, Sachs & Co. at the Conference Board discussions in November of 1971:

In my opinion no other career provides better training for a director's position. The breadth of corporate problems one sees—both financial and nonfinancial—in his daily work provides the investment banker invaluable insight and experience which can be very useful to a company on whose board he sits. Problem-solving ability and good judgment serve as important foundations in making an investment banker effective in his own business; they are skills which corporations should seek in directors.[4]

The same observations can be made about commercial bankers and lawyers. Both experience a wide range of situations in their careers that require the development of judgment and skills of a high order. In the case of lawyers, much can be said for electing to a board lawyers from firms which are not on regular retainers from the corporation. However, when the lawyer-director is a partner of the firm regularly retained by the corporation, he necessarily becomes, in the course of time, more like an officer of the company working under the chief executive officer. The responsibility to give completely objective advice in the best interest of the company can be difficult in these circumstances. Thus there is the potential for the lawyer-director to expose the company to the hazards of conflicts of interests and restriction of options similar to those created by the investment banker and the commercial banker. The relationship of the lawyer and of the accountant, respectively, to a company are not dissimilar, but it is interesting to note that members of accounting firms do not serve on the boards of the companies with which their firms have engagements.

These difficulties of conflicts of interests and the limitation of options can be minimized if care is taken. If it is not, many valuable directors from both law and finance

[4]Gustave L. Levy, "The Search for Greater Board Effectiveness - II," *The Board of Directors: New Challenges, New Directions*, p. 7.

may feel reluctant to make themselves available for election and a major source of talent would be less than fully utilized.

Former Corporate Officers

The most promising of all directions to look for an expansion of the pool of qualified directors, however, is to those who have had successful careers as corporate officers—and not necessarily in the company seeking board members. There is substance in the notion that business management has now acquired many of the characteristics of a profession. True, it has no commonly accepted entrance requirements, no formal certification examinations, no organized apprenticeship or internship. But each of these preparatory stages of the other professions is administered in its own way by the business organizations in which management careers are incubated. Pre-career preparation frequently involves four years of liberal arts education and perhaps one or two years in a broadly based program of graduate business study at a university. Institutions of higher learning, and many companies also, offer non-degree refresher periods of intensive study of management for corporate officers who are relieved of their daily assignments for the duration of this experience. There is now, "in the pipeline" of junior and middle management, a better prepared and larger number of potential senior executives, and eventually of board members, than at any previous time in the nation's history.

Few, if any, are now contemplating early retirement with the possibility of a second career as corporate directors. As a career objective it would be thought presumptuous and of doubtful attainability; and the limited appeal of the assignment under present circumstances could not be expected to call it to the attention of bright young men and women as a major goal to achieve, as a capstone to their careers. Yet as business corporations accept an enlarged participation in the common task to improve the quality of daily living, and as boards of directors acquire a more meaningful role in the guidance of corporations, a business career that progresses through the ranks to retirement as a senior corporate officer at fifty or fifty-five, with the potential of further service as a corporate director of one or several corporations, would have great appeal. It is completely natural that the professional manager should top off a career by serving as a professional director if his or her level of perception, knowledge of business, and breadth of vision qualifies for that position.

Summary answers can now be given to the remaining questions posed at the beginning of this chapter. The supply of those equipped to serve as members of working boards can be increased if the transition to the expanded requirements of time and talent occurs gradually and over a reasonable period of time. The supply is expansible and not static. The effort to cope with the social criticism of the corporation by extending board membership to those who would represent a special interest is both unpromising and undesirable. This is not, however, to say that non-business persons should be excluded from board membership. Bankers and lawyers can make excellent board members, but care must be exercised to avoid exposing them to conflict situations or restricting the company in its use of independent legal and financial resources. The growing practice of earlier retirement from operating responsibilities, in combination with an expanding number of trained executives in middle and senior management, provides a basis for anticipating an expanding number of eligibles for working boards in the years ahead. In a transitional period, simply because of the limited supply of those qualified with enough time to make the necessary commitment, it may be necessary to adopt arrangements similar to those now used by Texas Instruments. Selected senior officers are made officers of the board "retaining a reduced operating responsibility pending a complete withdrawal from management functions." Ultimately, it is desirable that all members of the board, including the chairman but not the chief executive officer, should be officers of the board only and not of the company. Apart from the chief executive officer, they should have no operating responsibilities.

The identification and election of the chairman of a working board presents a special situation. He would be the senior officer of the board—not of the company. The chief executive officer is the senior officer of the company and should report to the board as a whole—not directly to the chairman. The chairman and the chief executive officer should have their own duties. Obviously the chief executive officer and the chairman must be acceptable to each other. The most plausible source of a chairman is an early retired senior executive officer, but that need not inevitably be the case. Nor need it necessarily be the chief executive officer. The chief executive officer may be too valuable where he is, and his talents and interests may not fit comfortably with the role of the chairman. In that event, the board may wish to look outside for a chairman or to select another senior officer from the ranks of the company.

All members of working boards should have office space and secretarial and filing assistance to the extent needed. It should be provided by the company and be located near, but usually not in the same building, as the executive offices. Apart from this, the staff of the company should be used by board members for specific inquiries and investigations; but only after arrangements have been made for released time through the office of the chief executive officer. All board members should have access to the company's external as well as internal accounting and legal resources.

The amount of time that would be committed by a board member would depend on his specific assignments and would no doubt be conditioned by the extent of the challenges involved. If the board as a group is to fulfill the tasks described in this analysis of its role, all board members would have to spend more time than is now characteristic, and some board members very much more.

Attention should be paid to the physical convenience of board members when they are on company business, with the chairman or his executive secretary making the appropriate arrangements. Transportation and lodging should be matters of particular concern. Call it what you will, the "care and feeding" of board members is important to induce their maximum effort on behalf of the company, and a specific assignment of responsibility for attending to this matter as well as a modest budget should be arranged by the chairman.

7

Future Prospects of the Board of Directors

Several powerful influences are now exerting pressures to change the traditional position and practices of the governing boards of corporations. Countervailing influences resist any change that is more than nominal, but the probabilities seem to favor change that will become increasingly significant with the passage of time. Indeed, change has already begun as evidenced by the enormous increase of conferences, seminars, speeches, and monographs regarding governing boards, and more importantly, by the growing evidence of assertiveness by existing boards.

Change can occur in any one of numerous directions. This book describes one of those directions—a direction that has emerged from an attempt to apply rigorous logic in analyzing the basic legal position of the governing board, the needs of the corporation as they now exist and are likely to develop in the future, the personal talents and limitations of those charged with the guidance of the activities of corporations, and the reconciliation of the countervailing influences at play. The prescriptions proposed here will more than likely meet initial resistance at the highest levels of corporate officialdom. One can only hope that this resistance will decline after prolonged and mature reflection. What is involved here is a partial shift in authority within the governance of the corporation, an identification and division of functions between management and the board, and a progressive separation of management personnel from board personnel. More particularly, it has been proposed here that the respective assignments of the chairman and the chief executive officer be differentiated and assigned to different individuals. Without such changes, it is difficult to see how the board of the future can be organized to discharge fully the complex responsibilities required for the healthy development of the corporation and the security of board members from excessive liability.

The situation today is far from clear, despite the progress of recent years. The role of the governing board remains one of ambiguity, uncertainty, and doubt. It is not, for the present, a situation conducive to a total commitment to board work. Without considerable clarification and strengthening of their roles, members of governing boards cannot be reasonably expected to fulfill, to the extent of their capabilities, their inherent opportunities to contribute to the healthy future development of a corporation. Moreover, board members remain exposed to unnecessary personal liabilities. A number of recent cases in the federal courts have opened up—or have reopened— important questions as to the responsibilities and liabilities of directors and trustees. Not all of these questions will be settled easily or quickly. And a number of critics of the workings of large corporations have even questioned the legitimacy and efficacy of the institution of a governing board—at least as they see it. They point to the discrepancy between what boards do and what they are supposed to do, and question the procedures by which boards are recruited.

Even many directors and trustees themselves—and managers too—ask what *ought* the role of the board of directors in the large publicly held corporation to be? How *should* the board be constituted and organized? How *should* it work? Conscientious and thoughtful board members, however, probably more than judges on the bench or critics on the sidelines, are aware of the ambiguities, uncertainties, and doubts surrounding the board of directors or trustees of the large corporation, to say nothing of the tremendous diversity, from company to company and activity to activity, of the composition, workings, and plain effectiveness of boards.

Some who raise questions about the legitimacy of the boards of large corporations have suggested that boards should include representatives of the public, government, or special interest groups. These proposals have infirmities that could be seriously debilitating. Such measures would simply lead to political tension, or even to conflict where it has no real place. The business corporation has a *job* to do and should not be diverted by political wrangle. More specifically, such measures would make the board's role and function even more ambiguous than it is already.

Nevertheless, it must be conceded that everyone is interested in having our large institutions well run. And if we hope to sustain and even strengthen our voluntaristic private enterprise system, it must be recognized that corporations must ultimately achieve and retain a high level of public approval and sanction. And that approval, of course, must include acceptance of the board of directors as an institution. To that end, as well as for the purpose of contributing to the health and prosperity of large organizations, it is desirable that there be a clarification and public understanding of the role of the board.

It is with this goal in mind that the ideas presented here are designed to make governing boards and their structural organization effective and responsive to changing circumstances. A very important step in strengthening the position and role of the board is to make sure that it is *separate from the management*— both in function and in manning. The one exception here would be the chief executive officer of a corporation, who *would* serve as a board member, although in no case would he serve as the chairman of the board.

The Basic Distinction between the Board and Management

In this period of growing complexity, any brief identification of the role and responsibilities of directors would be an oversimplification. One basic distinction, however, may be regarded as essential to the effective discharge of the board's collective responsibilities for guiding the development, present and future, of all large organizations, particularly business corporations. It is: the governing board is the appropriate unit for the establishment of broad *policies* and *procedures* and for the review of *performance;* management is the agency delegated by the board to make those policies and procedures effective, subject to board review of performance. In the process of review, appraisal is made of *personnel* to whom authority for operations has been delegated. Correlatively, intervention by board members in the execution of policy, apart from prior approval and review, can be, and has proved to be, debilitating. It is not the function of the directors to run the organization from day to day, even though that meaning may lie on the surface of the language of the state charter.

A second major function of the board is to guide the organization in its dealings with the wide range of social issues which have been gathered under the rubric of corporate social responsibility and to which the public now expects all organizations, including business organizations, to be responsive. It is unfair to expect business management, whose success is measured by the return on investment, continuously to take actions that clearly increase costs and lessen profits without board encouragement and even initiative.

Something more should be observed about this second major function of the board. It would be less than effective to assign an initiating role in these external matters to the board without a concurrent strengthening of its involvement with management in the internal decision making of the corporation. The long-endured frustrations of many public relations departments bear adequate witness to the failure to do this. There have been any number of occasions in the past when a chairman of the board, divested of real influence in the internal activities of the company, has become "Mr. Outside"—with a rapid diminution of his credibility. If the chairman and his fellow board members are to be effective in representing the company to its many publics, there must be a recognition by the public that they speak for the whole board and that the board does, in collaboration with management, determine the organization's policy, and appraise personnel and performance.

Given these internal arrangements, the institution of the corporate board does have an unequaled opportunity to serve both the company and the world of business in general. Senator James L. Buckley made an interesting point at a recent conference:

... there is no challenge that the ingenuity of American business has not been able to meet except that of insuring the survival of the economic institutions that have provided our people with greater opportunities and a higher standard of living than have been enjoyed by any other society in history. [Yet,] ... executives ... tend to avoid the larger intellectual and political debates that together frame the direction of our society.[1]

This is understandable for several reasons. *Business Week* put it: "[The] Chief Executive: Facing outside forces for which he was neither trained nor selected".[2] Besides being fully occupied with running the business, there are risks of retaliation and public abuse from the political and journalistic communities when business executives espouse a point of view. Even though the position may be a sincere attempt to represent the public interest, it is often interpreted as a reflection of a narrow self-interest, and, unfortunately, all too frequently, the interpretation may have been correct. Credibility is hard for the business community to earn and retain.

A board of directors charged with initiating responsibilities for the external relations of a corporation and manned by persons with diverse talents and backgrounds, including—but not limited to—those of business experience and acumen, is much better positioned to win that credibility. Business has long needed articulate spokesmen who can convey the reality of business to the world of ideas in a manner that will capture the confidence of the public, who can make clear that an open society in the world of work and the world of politics are one and inseparable. There is no more natural or effective place to develop the required intellectual leader-

[1]Senator James L. Buckley, Speech to the Seventeenth Annual Business Conference, College of Business Administration, St. John's University, Hotel Commodore, December 5, 1974, p. 9.

[2]"The Chief Executive Officer," *Business Week,* May 4, 1974.

ship for business than in the governing boards of its major institutions.

The Transition to Separate Membership of the Board and Management

So that there will not be prolonged confusion about board and management functions, the objective of working toward a separation between membership on the board and membership in management should be established. At the present, people who have been and are intimately associated as executives with the activities of a large organization are often included on its board. This does have a good justification, for the activities of the large organization in business, in education, in medical care, and in philanthropy, including the financial aspects, are very complex. Considerable firsthand knowledge and experience with these aspects are indispensable. But having the executives with ongoing operating responsibilities and duties also serve as directors on the boards of these organizations is a source of ambiguity and confusion, and can operate to reduce the effectiveness of the board as an independent body. It is recognized, however, that, as a practical matter in particular cases, there must be a gradual transition of the officers involved from their operating responsibilities because of a limited availability of executive talent to man the vacated operating posts.

The common confusion between board and management can be avoided if, after joining the board, former officers of the management are relieved as rapidly as circumstances permit of all *operating* responsibilities. The one exception would be the president, whose principal function is managing the ongoing workings of the company and whose presence on the board is required both for his experience and to assure that board decisions can be properly understood, interpreted, and executed by management. A large part of the job of distinguishing the board and management can be accomplished by making sure that the chairman has *no* responsibility for day-to-day management, and that his sole job is to be, completely, the chairman of the board. If this is done, the occasion for confusion of roles simply cannot arise. But, when one individual serves as both chairman of the board and chief executive officer, there is the obvious difficulty of separating out the functions and responsibilities of the chief officer of the *board* from those which he has when he acts as chief executive of the *management*. Ambiguity of the role of the total board starts here. A sequential step to cure this confusion is to make sure that other executive officers below the president drop their operating assignments as quickly as possible.

There is nothing in this dichotomy of functions to imply conflict of purposes or adversary positions between the management and the board. On the other hand, arrangements that clarify the respective and separate functions and responsibilities of both board and management, and that provide a system of checks and balances between the two, will do much to minimize mistakes and maximize successes. It would also provide a new dimension to the effort of business to respond perceptively to the enlarged expectations of the public.

A New Concept of the Board Chairman

The distinction between board and management—the clear separation of the two—does imply a new and different concept of the role of the chairman of the board.

113

Although in most cases the chairman in a business organization would be elected by the board after a successful career in the company, the office would no longer be regarded as the reward for a job well done as chief executive officer. The talents and the interests required in the chairman's office are quite different from those of the office of the chief executive, and other senior personnel in the organization may be better qualified to be a board chairman. Indeed, the chairmen of not-for-profit organizations are recruited from a variety of careers in which they have demonstrated outstanding capabilities. In both cases, the chairman would become the senior officer of the *board*. The chief executive officer, that is, the president, would *not* report to the chairman directly but rather to the collective board, of which the chairman would be but one member.

The chairman's internal functions would be to organize the work of the board, which—certainly for most of our large, complex organizations—if done effectively would require a full-time or nearly full-time commitment. This would be especially true in the business corporation. In collaboration with the chief executive officer, the chairman would schedule, propose the agenda for, and organize regular and special board meetings; he would make a review of the adequacy of documentary material sent to other board members. Subject to the board's review, he would establish procedures to govern the board's work; he would keep the flow of information to board members under continuous review; he would assure adequate lead time for the effective study and discussion of matters under consideration; he would assign specific tasks to members of the board; and he would establish a committee structure to carry out the board's work.

Externally, he would serve as the principal bridge to

portray the company's activities to the public at large and, conversely, to interpret the significance of the political, sociological, and economic scene for the company's activities. Clearly this would require a wide range of interests and a high level of intelligence not typically found in a single individual. For the effective discharge of such heavy responsibilities, the chairman would necessarily need the support and perspective of fellow board members with wide experience and catholic concerns, including, of course, the practical and realistic concerns of the business. The chairman's posture, in other words, should have the quality of universality. The success of the duality of board and management would depend largely on his administration of the office. In addition, he should be prepared and equipped to take his place among the leaders of business thought and participate in the development of national public policy.

Board Committees: Their Commitments and Compensation

The legitimate functions and concerns of the board of directors of large, complex, often multinational business companies are so multifarious and difficult, and the burdens of handling them well so heavy, that special attention needs to be given to the task of setting up board committees and helping them to do their work properly without interfering with the ongoing work of management—and without being interfered with! In addition to the usual committees of finance, audit, conflicts of interests, compensation, personnel, and perhaps executive, some companies have committees concerned with technology and with public policy issues, but others feel that these are areas of interest to all members of the board. Whether or not to have these two committees or still

115

others, is a decision that is, and can be, made only in the particular context of each company.

Generally speaking, a greater participation by governing boards in the determination of policy and procedure, and in the review of personnel and performance, implies the commitment of much more time and attention than is the present practice of most directors and trustees of large organizations. Guidance in matters of corporate social responsibility imposes an additional dimension that is likely to grow in the demands it will make.

The greater participation advocated here certainly suggests a corresponding increase in compensation for board members. Indeed, the quality of board members and their work will be enhanced with a clarification of their functions and an increase in their remuneration. Those board members recruited from careers in the organization would be expected to retire from operating responsibilities at earlier ages, perhaps in their early or middle fifties. Membership on one or more boards would become a full-time career for some and a part-time career for most. Under such a system, the provision of adequate compensation for board members becomes especially important.

Board Independence

The search for greater independence and more positive commitment of board members has led some organizations to accept the notion of special interest representation from groups such as women, ethnic minorities, consumers, labor, environmentalists, etc. But it is not clear how the conflicting interests of multiple and diverse constituencies will, in the long run, be reconciled with the basic concern of the board, which is, of course, the survival and growth of the corporation. In the long run, a board consisting predominantly of members serving special interests could not be expected to maximize the development of the total activity. Rather, the current concern for interest group representation may prove to be more of an unstated recognition of the *need* for greater *independence* among all board members than a *solution* to the problem of independence.

It is more important to have a vigorous and informed review of the proposals that come before the board from the point of view of both the company and of the general interest than it is to have contending and specialized individuals on the board trying to represent the particular interests of limited constituencies. Conflict on the board would make effective action difficult. Service to a particular group may constitute a conflict of interests with the very institution that board members are elected to govern. Over time, the concerns of the several interests involved in the enterprise will be best served by the balanced and healthy *total* development of the enterprise as a whole.

That is not to say that specialized interests should go unsponsored. With a requisite degree of independence, *all* members of the board will feel a compulsion to take initiatives and espouse special causes from time to time, and not always the same cause. This is true of all who are worthy of board membership, regardless of sex, race, religious background, or other distinction. Indeed, there is a positive advantage in having board members with diverse experiences and backgrounds, who are capable of relating them to the corporate interest. The *character* of the individual is what is really paramount.

A reconceptualization of the governing board's functions and structure is a more promising way than constituency representation of assuring independence of its posture. Especially is this true of efforts to separate clearly the "legislative" functions of the board from the "executive" functions of the management and to establish and maintain as clear a demarcation as possible between the memberships of the two groups. Such steps should provide for the technical competence required in both bodies as well as for their ability to look at themselves and each other with objectivity. Those steps, alone, should do much to assure the "legitimacy" of the business corporation, its direction, and its management. They should also improve for all forms of organizations with governing boards the effectiveness and stability of the decision process.

Numerous books and articles, critical of the effectiveness of directors and trustees in the discharge of this or that aspect of their responsibilities, have appeared in recent years. Numerous community leaders are now persuaded that revitalization of the board of directors is urgently needed to assure the continued development of the large organization as a constructive influence in contemporary society. Although there is no single prescription for that revitalization, a major contribution to that important purpose can be made by a clarification and implementation of the respective functions of board members and of management, and this can best be achieved by a separation of their respective memberships.

8

Notes on Governing Boards of Not-for-Profit Corporations

THE corporate form is ubiquitous. It is used to achieve a wide range of private and public, profit and nonprofit, and governmental and government-related purposes in contemporary society. A variation of the chartered corporation is the organization created by a trust indenture. In terms of financial volume, the activity of the for-profit chartered corporation is by far the largest. In terms of the variety of organizations and purposes, the not-for-profit corporation which provides a service to the public without a profit, is the most numerous and the most rapidly expanding category. But all have governing boards.

In the absence of profit accrual, not-for-profit corporations rely on a variety of sources for their income, mostly from the sale of services. (1) Some, such as mutual insurance companies and savings banks, have a regular income that usually is sufficient to cover all costs and leave a margin for reserves. (2) Some, such as universities, hospitals, symphony orchestras, and museums, have a regu-

119

lar income from the sale of services that must be supplemented by gifts and the return from endowments to maintain their programs. (3) Some, the general welfare foundations, have a relatively large income from their endowments—perhaps occasionally supplemented by additional gifts—comparatively small operating expenses, and concern themselves with making grants to causes considered by their boards as worthy. (4) Others, such as the Red Cross, the Salvation Army, or the Council for Financial Aid to Education, make no or a small charge for their services, have no significant endowment income, and must rely on continuous giving for the maintenance of their programs. (5) Others, such as municipal power corporations, and metropolitan transportation and port authorities, have local, state, or federal government affiliations through which subsidies, if necessary, are provided to supplement income from the sale of their services. (6) And one must not forget the municipal and state institutions of higher learning. All of these not-for-profit corporations have governing boards whose members are either trustees, directors, or regents.

Even though this does not exhaust the list of not-for-profit corporations, it is sufficient to demonstrate the great variety of purposes served by them and to suggest the widely differing tasks of their governing boards and managers. Some brief observations on the roles of boards and directors in several of these types of nonprofit corporations will show both the similarities and contrasts with profit-making boards of directors.

Mutual Insurance Companies and Savings Banks

Appearances frequently fail to be reliable guides to reality. In the 1920s, a stock company in Canada, the Sun

Life Assurance Company, was a venturous and early purchaser of equities for its investment portfolio. Among its purchases were its own shares. Eventually, it acquired all of them, thereby becoming a mutual company with no outstanding stockholders to elect its governing board or to receive dividends. The nature of the company's business and the motivations of its management and governing board were little changed, if at all. Few companies have gone so far, but some have acquired large percentages of their outstanding shares for their own treasury or for their employee pension funds. *Plus ça change, plus c'est la même chose.*

Another illustration will demonstrate the subtlety of illusion. In 1844 a group of socialists in Rochdale, England, started a system of cooperative marketing in which credit was not given, but the "profits" were distributed at periodic intervals to customers in proportion to their purchases. It is interesting to consider that the largest corporation in the nation, the Metropolitan Life Insurance Company, has a pattern of operations similar to the Rochdale Associates. The main difference between them, apart from size, is the fact that the Metropolitan does extend credit to its customers in the form of policy loans. Its "profits" are distributed to its customers in reduced premiums or enhanced benefits. It has no stockholders to whom it pays dividends or who elect its governing board. Thus it is with all mutual companies; the motivation is not profits as such but rather improved service at less cost through heightened levels of efficiency. It is interesting that improved services at less cost through heightened levels of efficiency are also the means of achieving greater profits in a stock company.

Even though the basic economic goals may be similar for mutual companies and profit-making stock companies, the question remains whether or not the absence of profit motivation has resulted in a different relationship between the governing boards and managements. Does a distinguishable and significant difference result from the election of board members by stockholders, on the one hand, and by the policyholders or depositors, on the other? A brief examination of the relationship between boards and managements, as well as the duties and responsibilities of each, in mutual life insurance and savings banks discloses that it differs little from the relationship of the boards and managements of joint stock corporations.

The assets of mutual savings banks are in excess of $100 billion, and the assets of mutual insurance companies are much greater. Together with savings and loan associations and private pension funds, they constitute the main channel through which personal savings are gathered and made available for long-term capital investment. They are the heart of the long-term capital market—particularly the home mortgage market. Their primary economic function has been called "intermediation," i.e., the marshaling of the savings of many thousands of depositors and channeling them in to constructive investments in homes, factories, and other productive facilities.

Security more than risk-taking is salient in their operations, but that does not mean there is no room for the development of imaginative policies and administration. Competition among organizations to attract savings in the form of deposits or policy contracts is intense. Personnel training and motivation, site location, advertising, and the design of unique inducements for depositors and purchasers of policies are all parts of continuous efforts to acquire additional resources. The price paid to attract new savings is conditioned, in part, by the success with which the resources already acquired have been invested.

The degree of risk justified in the investment of assets by these organizations is measured by the nature of the present and future obligations to make payments. The mutual savings banks have long emphasized long-term mortgages in their investment portfolios; mortgages make up about 70 percent of their assets. Other fixed income securities may bring the total to 85 or 90 percent. Needless to say, the long-term trend in the value of real estate is a matter of prime interest to them. Mutual insurance companies have been more venturesome, committing a modest part of their portfolios to equities. The extent to which reserves are provided is another decision that requires judgment of a high order.

But even though the investment policies of mutual insurance companies and savings banks may be highly conservative, there are still major risks that require foresight in the management of assets. Variations in the money markets on at least four occasions in the last decade have resulted in net flows of funds out of the savings banks and mutual insurance companies. This happened when short-term interest rates rose significantly above the rates permitted by law on savings deposits and above the typical contractual 5 percent life insurance policy loan rate. This process of depositor and policyholder withdrawal is called "disintermediation." Returns of 5 to 6 percent cannot compete with the high 9 to 11 percent available in late 1974 on prime commercial paper, certificates of deposit, and other short-term liquid assets.

This brief description of the broad outlines of the activities of mutual savings banks and insurance companies is sufficient to disclose that many of the required decisions of a mutual company are comparable to those of corporations operating for profits. The activities involve marketing in its many aspects, including the "packaging" of service offerings to the public, real estate operations for its own account, and the allocation of resources among alternative investments. Personnel policies must be developed, and the mutual company must be sensitively aware of changes in the environment within which it functions.

Because of these similarities, we might expect that most of the comments made about the relations between governing boards and managements of profit-seeking corporations earlier would have approximate applicability to mutual companies. Indeed, the nature of the business and the size of the activity appear to be more important than the fact that a company is mutual and not-for-profit. The "four Ps" of profit-making corporate governing boards have equal applicability; the determination of *policy* and the review of *procedures* in the organization, participation in significant *personnel* matters and the audit of *performance* are no less important in the mutual company. Management succession should be no less a concern. Long lead times of three to five years are likewise desirable for the intensive, close appraisal of possible candidates to succeed incumbents in the office of the chief executive. The allocation of resources, the operating plan for a year ahead, and the development of the most efficient administrative structure are all matters that should have the board's attention, just as in a for-profit business. Potential conflicts of interests and executive compensation similarly require the attention of the board in a mutual company.

Whether the committee structure of the board of a mutual company should approximate that of the for-profit business corporation will again probably depend more on the size and the precise nature of the activity than upon other considerations. It must, of course, be adapted to the unique needs of the mutual company and kept as simple as possible in the interest of maximum efficiency. But, there is one difference that the boards of mutual insurance companies and savings banks might wish to recognize in the structure of their committees. In the case of the joint stock company, it was urged in an earlier chapter that all committees of the board and, indeed, the board as a whole should be concerned with issues of social responsibility. This was suggested to avoid the dilution of this concern by restricting it to a single committee charged with the review of the so-called externalities of the business. The mutual insurance companies and savings banks, however, have a unique and direct relationship to the environment in which they operate; it is the ultimate determinant of their success or failure.

The social as well as the economic character of the environment will shape their future opportunities. Intellectual ferment is now visible throughout the nation. Nontraditional values are being adopted. An awareness has emerged that past projections of population growth and economic expansion cannot be perpetuated. Life styles, including patterns of family life, are undergoing major changes. Two-thirds of the jobs available today are in the service industries, including government. More than 10 percent of personal incomes are now unrelated to individual contributions to production or to services rendered by the recipient; they are received from the government in the form of Social Security benefits, Medicare payments, unemployment compensation, veteran's benefits, and public aid. Fear of deprivation in the later years of life is no longer a major concern of youth. Environmental and quality-of-life issues have begun to displace maximum economic growth as the focus of public attention and public policy.

All of these matters will have a profound impact on the future operations of insurance and savings institutions. For example, they could determine the extent to which emphasis will be placed on forms of "contract savings" as opposed to continued primary reliance on "voluntary savings" to maintain volume. Because the externalities mentioned above are so inextricably woven into the long-range future of mutual insurance companies and savings banks, it may be that they should be given recognition and continuing analytical attention in a committee of the board solely for that purpose. Such a committee would necessarily be concerned with long-range development. Clearly, the personnel of such a committee, to be effective, must include those trained in the social and natural sciences as well as businessmen, lawyers, and financiers.

Colleges and Universities

The business of institutions of higher learning is dual in nature; to educate (i.e., to preserve and transmit knowledge) and to advance the fund of knowledge through research. Some would put the importance of these two functions in the order stated. Others would reverse it, particularly for those institutions that award advanced academic degrees. In recent years, a third function has begun to win some sponsors: participation in community action programs for the alleviation of social problems. This new job for the institutions of higher learning has by no means been fully accepted on the campus. There has been serious question in many minds whether involvement by universities and colleges in community problems may not be incompatible with the degree of objectivity required in a community of learning and research.

Colleges and universities are unique among corporate organizations in the variety of influences that bear on their activities. Centuries ago they started as clusters of scholars who individually admitted students to their classes for a fee. There was no administrative direction in those distant days, and faculties have continued to cherish the thought that their own limited legislative and administrative devices are quite adequate. On this view, the single function served by deans, vice presidents, presidents, and trustees is simply to keep the faculty nourished with adequate salaries, classrooms, offices, and research funds. Thus, it is reported that when General Eisenhower became President of Columbia University he admonished a faculty assembly to greater support of the university. "But, Mr. President," a senior professor rose to proclaim, "the faculty *is* the university."

There is much truth in the professor's statement, but it hardly implies that there is no role for academic and institutional administration. More than any other type of organization, a college or university presents two quite different sets of administrative tasks: what might be called academic administration, concerned with the scholarly program, on the one hand, and institutional administration, on the other. Departmental chairmen, deans, provosts, vice presidents for academic affairs, and presidents may be conceived as being in the line of academic administrators, working closely with faculty in the development and structure of scholarly activities. Directors of buildings and grounds, of food, and of other services, the registrar and other custodians of student and institutional records, the director of the budget, the treasurer, the vice president for government and public affairs, the vice president for development, and, yes, the chairman of the board and his board colleagues, all have responsibilities that are not essentially academic, even though they must be harmonized with the academic program.

Academic Administrators

Left alone, faculty members are understandably disposed to pursue their personal professional interests. But

127

often these are so specialized that they have little interest for students. The achievement of a balanced teaching program among the several academic disciplines, and even within departments concerned with a single discipline, would be unusual without administrative guidance. Without it, the result could readily be an extensive—and expensive—proliferation of specialized and sparsely attended course offerings.

There is, moreover, an unfortunate tendency among many intellectuals toward what has been called "bitchiness" and professional arrogance. Faculty fights are so verbally violent, it has been said, because the stakes are so low! Administrators must be available to mediate and reconcile. It is particularly important that administrators give encouragement in numerous ways to junior faculty members, who frequently feel impelled for the purpose of winning tenure to pattern their development after that of the senior professors in their departments. When this does happen, individuality suffers. That is one of the more subtle penalties of the faculty tenure system that is now under review throughout the nation.

There are numerous other academic administrative functions that must be carried out in managing a truly qualified program of higher learning. In addition to being financed, research leaves must be scheduled so that faculty is available to staff the program of course offerings for each semester and term. Schedules are constructed after student enrollments are estimated, the number and time of course offerings established, and the number of courses to be taught by each member of the available faculty has been determined. These are all matters that must be resolved within the limits of financial budgets that have been previously determined. In a large academic institution, such budgets require a lead time of not less than a year.

If a need develops for additional faculty members due to retirements, withdrawals for other reasons, or expanded enrollments, it is only natural that those most familiar with the work in a professional field initially identify the potential candidates. Even here, however, it is good to have the benefit of checks and balances provided by faculty colleagues in adjacent disciplines and by academic administrators.

The total intermeshing of functions presents an interesting problem in continuing logistics. And all of these procedures involve a high quantity of persuasion and consent in contrast to the greater emphasis on authority in the business corporation.

This brief recitation of the thoroughly integrated functioning between faculty and academic administrators will help to identify and emphasize two unique practices in the world of academe. First, academic administrators are usually chosen from the faculties, with little or no previous administrative experience. There is no precedent for a program of careful preparation for succession to important academic administrative posts. Second, an orderly program of career progression in academic administration is more the exception than the rule.

These practices are probably defensible when the administrator is in direct contact with the faculty, but they become less so to the degree that the administrative assignments are more removed from the academic program. Many contemporary universities and colleges have become large and enormously complex corporate organizations. Their annual budgets typically run into tens or even into hundreds of millions of dollars. The acquisition of resources and the development of the physical plant, the organization of an orderly system of operating and financial record keeping, and the task of representing the institution in its external relations, all are part of what we may here call institutional administration in contrast to academic administration.

Institutional Administrators

The tasks of institutional administration in colleges and universities are now enormously varied. A major task is the preservation of resources. The annual budget cannot be unbalanced indefinitely without incurring disaster. The endowment funds, if any, must be securely invested to provide income to supplement gifts and tuition fees. Tuition fees must be adjusted to reflect changing costs. Salary levels, both for the faculty and the administration, must be maintained at competitive levels. The physical properties must be maintained in good and attractive condition. Continuing decisions must be made in the allocation of available space to approved activities, financial resources must be allocated in directions of predetermined development, and even the intellectual resources represented in the faculties may be persuaded or cajoled to devote their energies and talents to purposes desired by those responsible for the directional development of the institution.

The assignment of faculty to institutional needs must necessarily involve mutual consent. It illustrates the importance of harmonizing institutional administration with the academic program. Thus, the activities of institutional administrators must be carefully tuned to the academic program, and, in turn, the academic program should be harmonized with the constrictions imposed by budgetary and other nonacademic circumstances. To the largest extent possible, academic considerations should prevail.

Many of the functions of institutional administrators are comparable to those of a business organization administrator, yet the procedures for picking most uni-

130

versity and college administrators today are simply an extension of those used to pick members of the teaching faculties. Reasonably successful in the latter case, they are often inadequate for selecting academic administrators, and may fail completely in picking institutional administrators. It is unrealistic to expect a professor whose career has been shaped by scholarly concerns to adapt quickly to the rigors and requirements for hard decisions involved in administering a multi-million dollar enterprise. Traditional methods that require no prior preparation for appointment to posts in institutional administration are unlikely to be successful. Excessive risks are incurred even when academic administrators are selected from the ranks of scholars by search committees without extended periods of observation.

––––––––––

Against this summary description of the operational life of institutions of higher learning, several observations may be made regarding the functioning of their governing boards. A significant modification must be made in the board's approach to the "four Ps" of policy, performance, personnel, and procedures that were identified in Chapter 2 as the focus of the business board's internal corporate interest.

Apart from trustee insistence upon the highest possible quality of teaching and scholarly work and the freedom for the faculty to inquire and express themselves, the academic *policy* of an institution of higher learning is a matter resolved by the interchange between faculty and academic administrators. Trustees have little to do with the precise patterns of the teaching and research programs, except to restrict their outer limits to available resources. Nor are trustees as well qualified to judge academic *performance* as are academic administrators and members of the faculty themselves. Moreover, most faculties have developed elaborate peer group arrangements, usually, but not always, including the participation of academic administrators, for the appraisal of scholarly personnel. Trustees can review nonacademic *performance and personnel* and, of course, should do so, but for trustees to attempt to inject themselves into the mystique of academe would be both foolhardy and frustrating.

The matter of reviewing *procedures,* both academic and nonacademic, throughout the institution is a more promising area for trustee attention. The procedures used by faculties for identifying new members of the teaching staff and appraising colleagues' professional progress in some cases do not eliminate bias and personality preferences. Objectivity is hard to achieve. Clarification of procedural relationships between the faculty and academic administrators could contribute to a more effective and harmonious community.

On the institutional or nonacademic side, there is a general need for better procedures to gather and disseminate operating and financial data. Its analysis and presentation in meaningful form, and its frequency of distribution, typically leave much to be desired. Without adequate and current data, the procedures for the allocation of space, money, and scholarly personnel can rest on no better base than intuitive judgment. And, procedures for finding, appointing, and developing nonacademic personnel could very profitably be given more careful attention. Indeed, perhaps the most fruitful field for university and college trustees to work is in the area of procedures.

In general, the most important function of college and university trustees is to keep the institution financially healthy. There are many things that can be done to tighten internal administrative procedures, but the major thrust must be to acquire additional and continuing sources of nourishment. Every member of the board should feel the obligation to participate in fund raising. The day has long since passed when universities and colleges could treat fund raising as a secondary activity to be assigned to a junior officer. The activity requires a daily commitment on the part of the senior officials of the institution—preferably by the chairman of the board and his fellow board members rather than the president, whose time and attention should be dedicated to the academic program and to representing the institution to the public and to academic associations.

Indeed, there is much to be said for making the chairman of the board a full-time trustee with an office on the campus and an appropriate salary. This would bring him into close proximity with the life of the institution, help him interpret its needs to potential donors, and facilitate his organization of the board in a manner which would best serve the interests of the college or university. As a full-time officer of the board, he would necessarily work in close harmony with the president, whose primary responsibility would be academic matters. He would also need a close association with the vice presidents for development and for business affairs.

If the principal functions of the governing boards of universities and colleges are related to the nonacademic aspects of these institutions, there is a serious question regarding the advisability of adding members from the faculties and from student bodies. The result can only be a confusion of the particular roles now respectively played by the component elements that make an institution of higher learning, but especially of the role of the board of trustees. Since neither students nor professors, as a rule, have any extensive experience in institutional administration, its supervision, or fund raising, their value on a board could not be high.

Hospitals

The administration of voluntary community hospitals involves as many subtleties and ambiguities as that of colleges and universities—perhaps even more. Initially organized as charitable institutions for the poor and managed by citizen boards of trustees or by a church, they have now become the workshops for physicians in practice and the focal point for both the delivery of sophisticated health care as well as general medicine to the poor. Unfortunately, their administrative structures and operating efficiencies have failed to keep pace with the growth of their medical skills and their social responsibilities.

A number of efforts have been made to "professionalize" hospital administration, but with limited success. Probably the most important reason for this is the anomalous organizational structure of hospitals with its built-in diffusion and ambiguity of authority. Staff physicians of a hospital are not typically employed by it but rather use its facilities with little or no responsibility for its efficiency or funding. Yet they have a major influence on the acquisition of equipment. The result is an inevitable degree of duplication and extravagance as competing hospitals equip themselves for prestige rather than need. Excessive facilities in many communities are said to have been developed in areas such as obstetrics, pediatrics, open heart surgery, and others.

Another reason for the inadequate administrative practices in hospitals has been the sheer increase in the rate of hospital development. Replacement of general medical practice by specialization has made the average medical specialist more dependent on the expensive facilities only the hospital can provide. In recent years the improvements have come rapidly. But unlike the situation in industry, investment in the instruments of our advancing

134

medical technology has not increased hospital efficiency and decreased costs; rather the reverse, it has increased costs in two respects: the capital commitment involved and the increased staff required to operate and service the equipment.

There are now some twenty people in the operating room for open heart surgery. The hospital work force per bed has nearly doubled in the last quarter-century. Moreover, the space needed has increased enormously. Formerly, a total of 300 to 400 square feet per bed, including operating rooms, nursing offices, etc., was thought to be adequate. Currently the figure is more like 700 to 800 square feet per bed. Improved medical equipment, resulting in higher per diem costs, have in many cases saved human lives. But the financial pressures on patients in hospitals have also risen tremendously with per diem costs of some $250 in the most specialized cancer hospitals.

Still another cause of the rapid growth in total expenditures that has made it so difficult for hospital administrators to cope is the growth of prepaid, group medical expense arrangements. Some Blue Cross–Blue Shield contracts may be validated only if the patient is hospitalized. The natural result has been an increased use of hospitals by patients. Twenty-five years ago, there was one admission annually for every ten in the population. Today the figure is one in every six. About two-fifths of charges for patient services are from public sources alone. With commercial and voluntary insurance covering much of the remaining hospital costs, there is little or no pressure on doctor or patient to economize. The process of collection itself involves an administrative task of some complexity; and it should be observed that inefficiencies are not only permitted but are positively invited by cost reimbursement formulas.

Unfortunately, hospital administration has not been a

135

field that has appealed to large numbers of talented people. Less than half of all hospitals are fortunate enough to have administrators with formal training. Perhaps a major reason is that there is no post comparable to a chief executive office. Nor can there be given the dual control of the medical staff and the lay board now characteristic of current practice. Perhaps one of the most effective means of increasing the attractiveness of the hospital administrator's post would be to make the incumbent an ex officio member of the governing board.

The current difficulties of the hospital administrator are summed up by noting that, although physicians are neither administrators nor employed by the hospital, they must necessarily make many decisions on how the resources of the hospital will be used, and even on what work the staff will do. On the other hand, the hospital administrator is buffeted by the realization that "the protective comforter of charitable enterprise" is gone and the hospital must now stand on its own in competition with other activities in the community. Thus, some of the most difficult labor demands of recent years have come from organized nurses and other nonprofessional members of hospital staffs.

The question in the title of Chapter 1, "Are Governing Boards Necessary?," can perhaps be answered more positively in the case of hospitals than of any other type of corporate organization. An urgent need for constructive action exists here, and the governing board seems to be the only place for it to begin. Yet little is heard of the activities of hospital trustees, and the general impression is one of lack of information, inattention, and indifference. No doubt there are many hardworking and thoughtful hospital trustees, and the image is probably only partially justified. A brief review of some of the opportunities available to the governing boards of hospitals will help to identify some of the constructive work that can be, and, in some instances, is being carried out.

An attempt to mitigate the consequences of dual control is perhaps the most important and the most challenging task for a hospital governing board. Physicians are not concerned with the administrative processes involved in data processing, purchasing, food sources, etc., but they are concerned with the results of those processes. They are deeply concerned with the range and quality of medical services, both diagnostic and therapeutic, provided by the hospital, but not with the necessary "housekeeping." But the housekeeping and the medical activities are inextricably intermingled, involve the hospital in expense, and both must be incorporated into periodic budgets if an orderly total operation is to be achieved. A few hospitals have experimented with making major departments into cost and profit centers in order to increase the involvement of the professional staff in controlling dollar outlays.

The board should insist that senior members of the medical staff, heads of departments, chiefs of clinical services, and the chief of staff join with administrators in the preparation of overall budgets projecting both income and expenses. The rules of the hospital should stipulate, with medical staff concurrence, that expenditures for specific activities will be restricted to agreed allotments approved by the board. Budgeting, moreover, can help trustees to make more exacting performance requests of both medical and nonmedical staffs. Indeed, it is desirable that the medical staff be adequately represented on the board, not so much as special pleaders for causes, but to assure that the medical staff is fully integrated into the overall conduct of the hospital. Transition from a system of dual control to one of integrated control through budgetary procedures is a complex task, probably involving many bruised sensibilities at first, but it is essential if the geometric progression of hospital costs is to be restrained. Only the board of governors can make it happen.

Intelligent budgeting requires data that accurately describe past operations and permit projections into the future. Hospitals are no better prepared to provide the required background information than are numerous other not-for-profit organizations. Improved information handling methods, including the use of computers, could contribute to better administrative control. Despite the difficulty of measuring the quality of health care, some uniformity in the collection of data among hospitals would provide a measure of comparative performance. Joint community action to eliminate unneeded overlaps of such things as outpatient services, specialized facilities, and other expensive activities would be facilitated.

The general level of motivation and competence in hospital staff personnel is another area for fruitful board attention. The development of such employee incentive plans as career ladders and merit pay programs may be a means of reducing employee turnover and provide inducements to increase productivity. In-service education to improve job performance against previously established work standards can improve motivation, especially if rigidity in work assignments is eliminated or relaxed. The increased use of paramedical personnel is both an inducement to achievement for employees and a source of economy in operations.

Much has been written about the key role expected of hospitals in the development of total health service programs in local communities. Comprehensive and coordinated health care systems have been envisaged that would also include neighborhood and group practice units, clinics, home and nursing-home care, and specialized care, such as dental, eye, ear, nose, and throat, and psychiatric treatment. To some extent, simply by virtue of the normal contacts that occur in a community, there is now a degree of collaboration that increases the accessibility of health service among these several dispensers of health care. The members of governing boards of hospitals can find further opportunities to avoid duplication through coordination, as has occurred in Rochester and Pittsburgh.

But if the concept of more formal coordination of health services with the hospital as the focus is ever to become a reality, the hospital must first get its own administrative house in better order. In the meanwhile, there may be other profitable opportunities to be examined by trustees, such as hospital mergers and new forms of service contracts to replace the disincentives inherent in cost-based reimbursement. Finally, trustees of hospitals, like those of universities and colleges, must never lose an awareness of the financial needs of the institutions they serve.

General Welfare Foundations

The grant-making general welfare foundation is simply an institutionalized form of charitable giving. Whether it increases—or decreases—the aggregate amount of philanthropy is probably impossible to determine. It is plausible to suppose that it increases the total by providing donors a means of identification and control as well as a means of continuing the donor's charitable goals beyond his life. Whether it increases the amount of giving for current use, however, depends in part on how much of the transfers to foundation endowments would otherwise have been donated for present needs.

The use of foundations for charitable purposes has a

centuries' old history, but an explosive growth in their size and number has occurred in the last fifty years. It is now estimated that there are in the United States some 26,000 general welfare foundations with $25 to $30 billion of endowment, making more than 500,000 annual grants totaling from $1.7 to $2.0 billion. Their size varies from the Ford and Johnson Foundations, each with several billion dollars of assets, to personal foundations with less than one hundred thousand dollars of assets.

The establishment of a foundation is a relatively simple matter accomplished by the execution of a living or testamentary trust. The trust indenture names the initial trustees, stipulates the nature of the goals to be sought, and the limitations within which the activities of the foundation may occur. Some indentures have set terminal dates by which all of the assets of the foundation must be distributed for the stipulated purpose or purposes. Indeed, in most cases, trustees of foundations could liquidate the corpus without such a stipulation, but that has not been a characteristic practice.

The deed of trust establishing a foundation typically names several trustees—usually the donor if it is a living trust, his lawyer, members of his family, and long-time friends and consultants. If the assets are of sufficient size, the trustees may feel the need to broaden the experience represented on the board and, perhaps, employ a director and staff. It is interesting to observe that before World War II very few foundations had paid staffs, and, even today, some foundations of considerable size have nothing more than clerical staffs that keep the books for audit and prepare tax reports. The trustees themselves in these cases review proposals, make the grants, and manage the investment portfolio.

Tax benefits that accrue to foundations have raised some knotty problems:

Foundations have come under fire in recent years as glorified tax loopholes and—far more threatening in a democracy—as private decision makers, substituting their judgment of what causes deserve to be helped for the public judgment represented by legislative appropriations.

The other side of the argument is, of course, . . . that the basic values of the foundations lie precisely in their ability to pioneer in areas barred to public agencies that must wait for a public consensus.[1]

Especially in the case of medium-sized and smaller foundations, there is a question of the degree to which donors should have the authority to name family and friends as trustees, and through self-perpetuation, to continue the family influence through successive generations. It is held that when monies are transferred from a private estate to a foundation corpus, they become essentially public monies, although they may be administered as a private trust. It has also been held that the privacy aspect should perhaps be interpreted to mean private persons dedicated to public purposes, which may or may not be true of the descendants. Opportunities for self-serving are not difficult to envisage.

Perhaps the most certain protection against the subtlety of this kind of abuse is the provision stipulated by several of the major donors of foundations in the past and implied in the 1969 Tax Reform Act, namely, that the assets of a foundation must be totally distributed after twenty to thirty years of existence. In addition to providing a degree of protection against abuse, this practice, if adopted by all foundations, would help to assure a certain amount of turnover among what have come to be known as "professional philanthropoids," thus bringing fresh thinking and purposes into the community of charitable giving.

[1]*Business Week,* December 7, 1974, pp. 92–3.

The principle of pluralism in society suggests that the more diverse the persons and groups involved in identifying social needs, the more varied the methods of decision-making; and the more dispersed the centers of decision, the more inventive and effective will be that society's approaches to the distribution of surplus wealth, the discovery of new knowledge, the maintenance of moral and spiritual traditions, and the conduct of significant human services.[2]

It is possible that setting a terminal date for the ultimate distribution of foundation assets would change the characteristic patterns of giving that now prevail. Today most foundation trustees and staffs regard gifts for the endowment of a recipient institution as inappropriate. The position is carried to the point of declining support for physical development and building funds. Most foundations are also reluctant to support ongoing activities that have proved their worth but need additional nourishment for their next stage of development. Rather, many foundations prefer the single grant—or perhaps a two-, three-, or five-year grant—with the idea that after such a grant the activity should have proved itself and made arrangements for other support.

These are all policies that express two guiding principles often heard in foundation circles: "We represent the venture capital of social change," and "Our task is to light fires and walk away; hopefully, they will attract the enthusiasm of others and continue to burn." Translated into foundation grant making this means that grants are usually made for newly conceived projects, largely in the area of research. There can be no doubt that the general welfare foundation, free of the constraints found in many other institutions, is ideally suited to encourage a penetration of the frontiers of knowledge. The foundation is

[2]*Report of the American Assembly,* Great Lakes Assembly on the Future of Foundations, Illinois Beach Lodge, Zion, Illinois, September 12–14, 1974, p. 4.

also well suited to induce a certain amount of social change.

These were policies that were set several decades ago by two or three of the great foundations. They have now been emulated by the many newer foundations during a period when annual grants have grown from some $200 million to the present level of approximately $2 billion. But it is one thing to have some $200 million of grants a year, mostly for new projects, and quite another thing when the total of new project grants is increased by a factor of ten. Foundation trustees may not have weighed with sufficient care the amount of negative disruption in the reassignment of intellectual personnel created by new project grants intended to benefit the public good.

The large growth of foundations in combination with the characteristic patterns of their grants has had several consequences. Large estates, which at one time were given or left to the trustees of favorite institutions of higher learning, hospitals, or museums to administer, have increasingly been placed in trust for foundation administration. Instead of supporting ongoing activities, the income from foundation endowment is diverted to newly designed projects. Originality on the part of the foundation staff, the expenses of which may absorb some 8 to 10 percent of the endowment income, has become a measure of its success.

The shift of monies from one use to another is not the only transfer. There is a limited supply of truly qualified talent to staff our colleges, universities, hospitals, and museums, and, to the extent that it is removed from its normal activities within these institutions, by reassignment to work on projects newly inspired and financed by foundations, the supply is further reduced. Another and more subtle transfer is the shift in the locus of decisions regarding programs in colleges and universities from the administrators and trustees of educational institutions to the staffs and trustees of foundations. The ability to dispose of grant money in large amounts is accompanied by influence, whether willed or not.

These are some of the broad philosophical questions that should concern the trustees of foundations. They override in importance the supervision of staff and the operating procedures of daily activities. Yet these administrative matters are consequential and cannot be neglected. The procedures for screening grants is the most important. Thus, should foundation staffs, where they are employed, report all proposals received to the board or just those that they recommend for approval? Should the staff provide an explanation of why a request did not receive their approval? Should the staff and trustees seek out proposals for predetermined purposes from possible recipients? Should a foundation make a few significant grants and see them through, hopefully to a successful conclusion? Or is a greater good likely to result from scattering a large number of modest grants in the hope of discovering new talents? How much monitoring by staff of performance by recipients of grants should the board expect? Should reports of results be made to the public at large as well as to the board?

All these questions should be answered in terms of achieving a greater participation by the trustees in the foundation decision process. All too frequently, the agenda for a foundation board meeting will consist of a specific set of recommendations by the staff for action, to which the board simply reacts, positively or negatively—usually the former. The total process of the foundation is thus basically molded more by the staff than by the board. A committee of the board charged with overall policy and program review could provide a counterbalance to the bias that is hard to avoid in most existing procedures.

In addition to these questions dealing with the basic grant function of the foundation, the board must be concerned with the more mundane matters of record keeping, auditing of the books, budget control, and tax reports, a task becoming more complex with each successive legislative act. These are all staff functions that require review by the board. But there is another administrative task that the board would be well advised to initiate on its own. As is the case with business organizations, conflicts of interests and acts of self-serving sometimes occur among members of both staff and board in a foundation's operations. A committee of the board should have this matter under continuous review.

Conclusions

This brief review of the opportunities and work of governing boards of not-for-profit organizations, i.e., mutual business corporations, institutions of higher learning, hospitals, and general welfare foundations, has pointed out both similarities with and differences from the governing boards of joint stock business corporations. The differences turn out to stem more from the fields of activity that nonprofit corporations pursue as contrasted with those of for-profit corporations than from the absence of the profit motive.

The procedures for the appointment and termination of board members should not vary significantly from those in business corporations despite the absence of stockholder proxy arrangements. All boards of directors are becoming increasingly concerned about and involved with the rapid changes occurring in the social environment. The catechism of the "four Ps" for governing boards, of policy, procedures, performance, and personnel, applies to all boards but with different emphases depending on the nature of the organization's activity. For example, academic personnel and performance touches the university or college board only peripherally through budgets; and the same is true of medical personnel and performance in hospitals. In both academic and medical organizations, financial and administrative procedures and performance are prime considerations of the governing boards. While policy considerations may be the most pronounced in the case of the general welfare foundation, they are also of high importance for all boards' attention. And of course, no board can be unaware of the importance of monitoring the potential for conflicts of interests in situations that involve significant resources. A sense of commitment, whether based on pecuniary reward for the board member or on the satisfaction and prestige of public service, should be an essential prerequisite of election to any governing board, whether the organization is for-profit or not-for-profit.

Bibliography

Books and Reports

BAKER, JOHN C. *Directors and Their Functions.* Boston: Graduate School of Business Administration, Harvard University, 1945.

BARNARD, CHESTER I. *The Function of the Executive.* Cambridge: Harvard University Press, 1938.

BERLE, ADOLF A., JR., and MEANS, GARDINER. *The Modern Corporation and Private Property,* rev. ed. New York: Harcourt, Brace & World, 1968.

BLUMBERG, PHILLIP I. *Corporate Responsibility in a Changing Society.* Boston: Boston University School of Law, 1972.

BROWN, COURTNEY C., and SMITH, EVERETT E., eds. *The Director Looks at His Job.* New York: Columbia University Press, 1957.

BUCHANAN, SCOTT. *Essay on Politics.* New York: Philosophical Library, 1953.

BUCHANAN, SCOTT. *The Corporation and the Republic.* New York: Fund for the Republic, 1958.

CHAMBERLAIN, NEIL W. *The Limits of Corporate Responsibility.* New York: Basic Books, 1973.

COPELAND, MELVIN T., and TOWL, ANDREW R. *The Board of Directors and Business Management.* Boston: Graduate School of Business Administration, Harvard University, 1947.

DAUGHEN, J. R., and BINZEN, P. *The Wreck of the Penn Central.* Boston: Little, Brown & Co., 1971.

DAVIS, JOHN W. *Corporations.* New York: Capricorn Books, 1961.

DE HOGHTON, CHARLES, ed. *The Company: Law, Structure and Reform in Eleven Countries.* New York: Macmillan Co., 1969.

DEWEY, LLOYD E. "The Board of Directors," in J. I. Bogen, ed. *Financial Handbook,* 3rd ed. New York: Ronald Press Co., 1956.

DRUCKER, PETER F. *The Concept of the Corporation,* 1946. New York: John Day Co., 1972, with a new preface and an epilogue.

DRUCKER, PETER F. *The Practice of Management.* New York: Harper & Row, 1954.

EELLS, RICHARD. *The Government of Corporations.* New York: Free Press of Glencoe, 1962.

General Electric Company. *Survey of Boards of Directors — Practices and Procedures.* New York: 1969.

GREENLEAF, ROBERT K. *Trustees as Servants.* Cambridge, Mass.: Center for Applied Studies, 1974.

HEIDRICK and STRUGGLES. *The Director.* London: October, 1971.

Investor Responsibility Research Center. *Cumulative Voting for Directors,* Special Report No. 3. Washington, D.C., April 11, 1973.

Investor Responsibility Research Center. *How Institutions Voted on Shareholder Resolutions,* 1973, Special Report No. 5. Washington, D.C., July 8, 1973.

JACKSON, PERCIVAL E. *What Every Corporate Director Should Know.* New York: William-Frederick Press, 1957.

JACOBY, NEIL H. *Corporate Power and Social Responsibility: A Blueprint for the Future.* New York: Macmillan Publishing Co., 1973.

JURAN, J. M., and LOUDEN, J. KEITH. *The Corporate Director.* New York: American Management Association, 1966.

KOONTZ, HAROLD D. *The Board of Directors and Effective Management.* New York: McGraw-Hill, 1967.

LOUDEN, J. KEITH. *The Effective Director in Action.* New York: American Management Association, 1975.

MACE, MYLES L. *The Board of Directors in Small Corporations.* Boston: Graduate School of Business Administration, Harvard University, 1948.

MACE, MYLES L. *Directors: Myth and Reality.* Boston: Division of Research, Graduate School of Business Administration, Harvard University, 1971, chap. 9.

MASON, EDWARD S., ed. with an Introduction. *The Corporation in Modern Society.* Cambridge: Harvard University Press, 1959.

McDavitt, Clarence G. *If You're a Bank Director.* Boston: Bankers Publishing Co., 1959.

Mueller, Robert Kirk. *The Board Life: Realities of Being a Corporate Director.* New York: Amacon, 1974.

Mueller, Robert Kirk, ed. *The Corporate Director: New Roles—New Responsibilities.* Boston: Cahners Books, 1975.

Nader, Ralph, and Green, Mark J. *Corporate Power in America.* New York: Grossman Publishers, 1973.

Securities and Exchange Commission. *Institutional Investor Study Report,* 5 vols. Washington, D.C., March 10, 1971.

The Conference Board. *The Board of Directors: New Challenges, New Directions,* A Conference Report from the Conference Board, November 18, 1971. New York: The Conference Board, 1972.

The Conference Board. *Corporate Directorship Practices: Compensation,* A Joint Research Report from the Conference Board and the American Society of Corporate Secretaries, Inc. By Jeremy Bacon. New York: The Conference Board, 1973.

The Conference Board. *Corporate Directorship Practices: Membership and Committees of the Board,* A Joint Research Report from the Conference Board and the American Society of Corporate Secretaries, Inc. By Jeremy Bacon. New York: The Conference Board, 1973.

The Conference Board. *Corporate Directorship Practices: Role, Selection and Legal Status of the Board,* A Joint Research Report from the Conference Board and the American Society of Corporate Secretaries, Inc. By Jeremy Bacon and James K. Brown. New York: The Conference Board, 1975.

U.S., Congress, House of Representatives, Committee on Banking and Currency. *The Penn Central Failure and the Role of Financial Institutions,* Staff Report, 92d Cong., 1st sess., January 3, 1972 (Washington, D.C.: Government Printing Office, 1972), pp. vi, ix.

U.S., Congress, Senate, Finance Committee. *The Role of Institutional Investors in the Stock Market.* July 24, 1973.

U.S., Congress, Senate, Finance Subcommittee on Financial Markets. *Financial Markets: The Impact of Institutional Investors in the Stock Market,* Hearings, July 24–26, 1973.

Vance, Stanley C. *The Corporate Director: A Critical Evaluation.* Homewood, Illinois: Dow Jones-Irwin, 1968.

Votaw, Dow. *Modern Corporations.* Englewood Cliffs, N.J.: Prentice-Hall, 1965.

Articles

ANDREWS, KENNETH R. "Can the Best Corporations Be Made Moral." *Harvard Business Review*, vol. 51, no. 3, May–June, 1973.

BLOUGH, ROGER M. "The Outside Director at Work on the Board." *The Record of the Association of the Bar of the City of New York*, vol. 28, no. 3 (March 1973).

BLUMBERG, PHILLIP I. "Reflections on Proposals for Corporate Reform Through Change in the Composition of the Board of Directors: 'Special Interest' or 'Public Directors.'" *Boston University Law Review*, vol. 53, no. 3 (May 1973).

Business Week. "The Board: It's Obsolete Unless Overhauled." May 22, 1971.

Business Week. "Institutions that Balk at Anti-Social Management." January 19, 1974.

Business Week. "The Chief Executive Officer." May 4, 1974, *passim*.

CAPLIN, MORTIMER M. "Shareholder Nominations of Directors: A Program for Fair Corporate Suffrage." *Virginia Law Review*, vol. 39, no. 2 (February 1953).

CARSON, LESTER. "Black Directors." *Black Enterprise* (September 1973).

CARY, WILLIAM L. "Federalism and Corporate Law: Reflections Upon Delaware." *Yale Law Journal* (1974).

DODD, E. M., JR. "Company and Corporation Law." *Encyclopedia Britannica*, 1958 ed., vol. 6, p. 150.

DOUGLAS, WILLIAM O. "Directors Who Do Not Direct." *Harvard Law Review*, 47 (1934): 1305.

EISENBERG, MELVIN A. "Access to the Corporate Proxy Machinery." *Harvard Law Review*, 83 (1970): 1489.

EISENBERG, MELVIN A. "The Legal Roles of Shareholders and Management in Modern Corporate Decision Making." *California Law Review*, vol. 57, no. 1 (January 1969).

ESTES, ROBERT M. "Outside Directors: More Vulnerable Than Ever." *Harvard Business Review*, vol. 51, no. 1, January–February, 1973.

ETHE, SOLOMON, and PEGRAM, ROGER M. *Corporate Directorship Practices*, Studies in Business Policy, No. 90. New York: National Industrial Conference Board, January, 1949.

GOLDBERG, ARTHUR J. "Debate on Outside Directors." *New York Times*, October 29, 1972.

HENNING, JOEL F. "Federal Corporate Chartering for Big Business: An Idea Whose Time Has Come?" *De Paul Law Review,* 21 (1972): 915.

KOONTZ, HAROLD D. "Should There Be Special Interest Representation on Boards of Directors?" *Business Horizons,* Winter, 1972.

MANNING, BAYLESS. "The American Stockholder: A Review." *Yale Law Journal,* 67 (1948).

SCHWARTZ, DONALD E. "A Plan to Save the Board." *The Record of the Association of the Bar of the City of New York,* vol. 28, no. 5 (April 1973).

SCHWARTZ, DONALD E. "The Public-Interest Proxy Contest: Reflections on Campaign GM." *Michigan Law Review,* vol. 69, no. 3 (January 1971).

SCHWARTZ, DONALD E. "Toward New Corporate Goals: Coexistence with Society." *Georgetown Law Journal,* vol. 60, no. 1 (October 1971).

SMITH, E. EVERETT. "The Goldberg Dilemma: Directorships." *Wall Street Journal,* February 7, 1973.

VAGTS, DETLEV F. "Reforming the 'Modern' Corporation: Perspectives from the German." *Harvard Law Review,* 80 (1966): 23.

VAGTS, DETLEV F. "The European System." *The Business Lawyer,* February, 1972, p. 165.

VANDERVICKEN, PETER. "Change Invades the Board Room." *Fortune,* May, 1972.

WEINBERG, SIDNEY. "A Corporation Director Looks at His Job." *Harvard Business Review,* vol. 27, no. 5 (September 1949).

Speeches

CONNOR, JOHN J. "An Alternative to the Goldberg Prescription." Remarks to the American Society of Corporate Secretaries, March 14, 1973.

CABOT, LOUIS W. "Directorships at the Crossroads: Collaboration or Confrontation." Remarks of the Chairman of the Cabot Corp. to stockholders of the Federal Reserve Bank of Boston, October 18, 1973.

SOMMER, A. A., JR., Commissioner, Securities and Exchange Commission. "Directors and the Federal Securities Laws," Address of February 21, 1974.

Index

Index

Index

Courtney C. Brown

DR. COURTNEY C. BROWN is Dean Emeritus and Paul Garrett Emeritus Professor of Public Policy and Business Responsibility of the Graduate School of Business of Columbia University. He is currently Chairman of the Board of Directors of the American Assembly.

Born in 1904, in St. Louis, Missouri, he was educated at Dartmouth College and did graduate work in economics at Columbia University. During World War II, he served with the Department of State and the War Food Administration in negotiations with other countries to procure their exportable surpluses of supplies needed by the Allies. Following the war, he was associated with the Standard Oil Company (New Jersey) as Chief Petroleum Economist and Assistant to the Chairman of the Board.

Dr. Brown has had long personal experience with the boards of both business and charitable corporations. He has served on the boards of directors of Esso Standard Oil Company, American Standard, American Electric Power, Uris Buildings, and the New York Stock Exchange. At the present, he serves on the boards of Associated Dry Goods, the Borden Company, the Columbia Broadcasting System, Union Pacific, and the West Side Advisory Board of the Chemical Bank. He serves on the Executive Committee of three of these companies, and as Chairman of the Finance Committee of one, the Audit Committee of another, the Conflict of Interests Committee of a third, and the Executive Compensation Committee of a fourth.

His experience on the boards of not-for-profit corporations is equally wide, having served on the boards of the Interracial Council for Business Opportunity and the New York Advisory Board of the Salvation Army. Currently, he is a member of the boards of the American Assembly, the International Executive Service Corps, and the Academy of Political Science. He is a honorary director of the Council for Financial Aid to Education (which he assisted Alfred P. Sloan, Irving Olds, and Frank W. Abrams to found in 1952).